THE MIGHTY ACTS OF JESUS ACCORDING TO MATTHEW

By BIRGER GERHARDSSON

WIPF & STOCK · Eugene, Oregon

Wipf and Stock Publishers
199 W 8th Ave, Suite 3
Eugene, OR 97401

The Mighty Acts of Jesus According to Matthew
By Gerhardsson, Birger
Copyright©1979 by Gerhardsson, Birger
ISBN 13: 978-1-4982-9251-1
Publication date 2/24/2016
Previously published by CWK Gleerup, 1979

Translated by Robert Dewsnap

Preface

This study is dedicated to the memory of *Bishop Gustaf Aulén*, who would have reached the age of 100 on 19th May, 1979. My subject has no *specific* connection with Aulén's own life work as a scholar and theologian. And yet it is still fully appropriate for a study in his memory. All his life he was deeply interested in scholarly investigations of every aspect of religious studies, as he was indeed by all research into human life. And during the last decades of his long life he evinced a particular love for New Testament scholarship. The chief testimony to this is his book *Jesus in Contemporary Historical Research* (1976; Swedish original, 1975). Therefore I know that my subject would have been of the greatest interest to him. It is with gratitude and pleasure that I write this dedication.

Birger Gerhardsson

Contents

Introduction 7

1. The general terminology 11
   1.1. *Teras* 11
   1.2. *Sēmeion* 12
   1.3. *Thaumasion, paradoxon, endoxon, ergon* 15
   1.4. *Dynamis* 16
   1.5. Concluding remarks 17

2. The summarizing accounts of Jesus' therapeutic activity in Israel .. 20
   2.1. The material 20
   2.2. The persons 21
   2.3. The individual summaries 22
   2.3.1. The programmatic summaries in 4:23—25 and 9:35 22
   2.3.2. The summaries with formula quotations 24
   2.3.2.1. The summary in 8:16(—17) 24
   2.3.2.2. The summary in 12:15—16(—21) 25
   2.3.3. The preludes to the feeding stories 27
   2.3.3.1. The introduction to the first feeding story, 14:13—14 27
   2.3.3.2. The introduction to the second feeding story, 15:29—31 ... 28
   2.3.4. The remaining summaries 28
   2.3.4.1. The summary in 14:(34—)35—36 28
   2.3.4.2. The summary in 19:1—2 29
   2.3.4.3. The final summary, 21:14(—17) 29
   2.3.5. The "quasi-summaries" 30
   2.3.5.1. Jesus assigns the disciples their task, 10:1, (5—)7—8 30
   2.3.5.2. Jesus' answer to John, 11:(2—)4—6 31
   2.4. Jesus' therapeutic actions 32
   2.5. The diseases 34
   2.6. The places 34
   2.7. Concluding remarks 36

3. The pericopes of Jesus' therapeutic miracles in individual cases ... 38
   3.1. The material 38
   3.2. The collection in chapters 8—9 39
   3.3. The form 40
   3.4. The diseases 42
   3.5. The persons 42
   3.6. The principal themes of the pericopes: the *exousia* of Jesus and the faith of men 45
   3.7. Further aspects of the question of faith 49

4. The pericopes of Jesus' non-therapeutic miracles 52
   4.1. The material 52
   4.2. The form 53
   4.3. The persons 53
   4.4. The individual pericopes 54
   4.4.1. The calming of the storm, 8: 23—27 54
   4.4.2. (a) The feeding of 5 000 men, 14: 13—21 55
          (b) The feeding of 4 000 men, 15: 29—39 55
   4.4.3. (a) The walking on the sea, 14: 22—33 57
          (b) Peter's walking on the water, 14: 28—31 57
   4.4.4. The cursing of the fig tree, 21: 18—22 58
   4.4.5. The coin in the fish's mouth, 17: (24—)25 b—27 59
   4.5. The main theme of the pericopes: the *exousia* of Jesus and the disciples .. 60
   4.6. Faith 62
   4.7. Comparison with the therapeutic miracles 65

5. Material concerning resistance and controversies 68
   5.1. The material 68
   5.2. Unreceptiveness and rejection 68
   5.2.1. The unreceptiveness in Nazareth, 13: 54—58 69
   5.2.2. The unreceptiveness in Chorazin, Bethsaida and Capernaum, 11: 20—24 71
   5.3. The adversaries' polemics 72
   5.3.1. The controversies on the exorcisms, 9: 32—34, 12: 22—32 73
   5.3.2. The controversy on the forgiveness of sins, 9: 1—8 75
   5.3.3. The controversy over healing on the sabbath, 12: 9—14 77
   5.4. Some conclusions and reflections on the controversy situation .. 79

6. The Christological appellations in our material 82
   6.1. Jesus, the Christ, "the Coming One" 82
   6.2. The Son of Man 83
   6.3. The Lord (*Kyrios*) 85
   6.4. The Son of David 86
   6.5. The Son of God and the Servant of God 88
   6.6. Concluding remarks 91

Conclusion: The mighty acts of Jesus according to Matthew 93

Introduction

During the last few decades, research into the New Testament texts on the miracles of Jesus has been advanced by many different types of investigation. Some of these studies have been directed towards a definite text, a certain theme or a specific aspect of the intricate complex of problems with which our sources present us. Some have been made from generally semiotic and structuralist points of departure, and these have attracted considerable attention.[1] Others have attempted to cover many aspects. I am thinking in particular of Gerd Theissen's *Urchristliche Wundergeschichten* (1974),[2] a work that is unusually rich in substance. Others again have attempted to show the characteristic features of the presentation of the miracles of Jesus given in the individual gospel.[3] As far as the Matthean perspectives are concerned an early work must be mentioned which has rightly assumed a dominant role. This is Heinz Joachim Held's excellent investigation *Matthäus als Interpret der Wundergeschichten* (1960).[4] For my own part I particularly wish to acknowledge my debt of gratitude to the investigations of Held and Theissen.

The study I present here is part of the preliminary work for a coming commentary on the Gospel of Matthew. This explains its character: it is not complete and not carefully rounded off; it is limited to certain aspects. And these are of a general nature. I classify the material, examine the form and characteristic peculiarities of the various groups of material, the persons appearing, the main points and main tendencies and so forth.

---

[1] For literature, see X. Léon-Dufour (ed.), *Les miracles de Jésus selon le Nouveau Testament*, Paris 1977, 151—181 (J. Calloud, G. Combet, J. Delorme), and *Semeia 11*: Early Christian Miracle Stories (ed. R. W. Funk), Missoula 1978.

[2] *Urchristliche Wundergeschichten. Ein Beitrag zur formgeschichtlichen Erforschung der synoptischen Evangelien*, Gütersloh 1974. For criticism, cf. e.g. *Semeia 11*. See also C. F. D. Moule (ed.), *Miracles. Cambridge Studies in their Philosophy and History*, London 1965, and Léon-Dufour, *op. cit.*

[3] As to the miracles in Mark, see K. Kertelge, *Die Wunder Jesu im Markusevangelium. Eine redaktionsgeschichtliche Untersuchung*, München 1970, L. Schenke, *Die Wundererzählungen des Markusevangeliums*, Stuttgart 1975, D.-A. Koch, *Die Bedeutung der Wundererzählungen für die Christologie des Markusevangeliums*, Berlin & New York 1975. For the miracles in Luke and John, see below, chap. 1, notes 5 and 15 (=1: 5, 1: 15) respectively.

[4] In G. Bornkamm, G. Barth, H. J. Held, *Überlieferung und Kirche im Matthäusevangelium*, Neukirchen-Vluyn 1960, 1976[7]. I have used the fourth edition.

My work consists of what may be called a synchronic examination of the material in the Gospel of Matthew as we have it. Despite my great interest in the Old Testament, Jewish and Hellenistic background of the early Christian material, I hardly go into this at all. In my analysis of the Matthean texts, I only occasionally and only very briefly hint at the genetic problems — the questions of the historicity of the events, the traditio-historical problems of our material, the relationship between the synoptic gospels and the like.

As far as the questions of historicity are concerned, it would be foolhardy to try to solve these by a study of the Gospel of Matthew alone. The remaining gospels — like all the other relevant source material — must of course be taken into consideration.[5]

The history of this material's tradition requires an amount of space that is not at my disposal. I have most recently sketched out my views in broad outline in the small volume *The Origins of the Gospel Traditions* (1979).[6] In the study here presented I only have reason to deal with the final result of the "work with the word" of the Matthean circle.

In recent years the debate concerning the synoptic question has been problematized in various ways, not least through the efforts to revive the Griesbach hypothesis and the attempts to show multifold, complex relations between the material in the synoptic gospels. I myself believe that complex solutions must be resorted to, while paying attention to the interplay of oral and written tradition. However, the work with the miracle narratives in the Gospel of Matthew has not in any way altered my view — by no means a dogmatic one — of the course of the tradition or my view — a relatively open one — of the priority of the Gospel of Mark to that of Matthew. In many of my arguments the fundamental opinion will be noticed that Matthew has used the Gospel of Mark. In general, however, I make no pronouncements on the questions of relationship. By the expression "the Marcan material" I mean merely the material which Matthew has in common with Mark, and by "the Q material" I mean the material which Matthew and Luke have in common over and above the Marcan material.

As is apparent from the title of this book, I am not writing about all the miracles in the Gospel of Matthew but only about the mighty acts which *Jesus* is said to perform (and which his followers perform in his name). I do not take up the miracles which happen to him (the virgin

---

[5] On the question of historicity, cf. e.g. R. Pesch's well-known book *Jesu ureigene Taten?*, Frieburg, Basel & Wien 1970. For literature about the wider, systematic discussion of the miracle question, see most recently B. Bron, *Das Wunder. Das theologische Wunderverständnis im Horizont des neuzeitlichen Natur- und Geschichtsbegriffs*, Göttingen 1975.

[6] Philadelphia 1979. The Swedish original has the title *Evangeliernas förhistoria* (Lund 1977).

birth, the resurrection, the epiphanies of the baptism and transfiguration, and the like).

In previous contexts [7] I have attempted to demonstrate how Matthew sees the activity of Jesus in Israel as a ministry in two phases: first in "strength" and then in "weakness". All his mighty acts belong to the first of these two phases: when he stands under the divine "blessing", when he is allowed to receive his destiny from the "measure of goodness" of God. It is within this total perspective that I examine the Matthean statements on the mighty acts of Jesus in Israel.

---

[7] See my article Gottes Sohn als Diener Gottes. Messias, Agape und Himmelsherrschaft nach dem Matthäusevangelium, *Studia Theol.* 27 (1973), 73—106. The thesis is already adumbrated in Jésus livré et abandonné d'après la passion selon Saint Matthieu, *Rev. Bibl.* 76 (1969), 206—227.

1. The general terminology

To make it possible to gain a grasp of how Jesus' mighty acts are portrayed in the Gospel of Matthew it is — I think — of interest to make some study of the terminology.[1] We shall therefore begin with some facts and reflections concerning the summarizing terms: which terms were within reach for Mark, Matthew and Luke, and which of these did they employ — either by way of exception or *par préférence*? Matthew's use of language appears to be fairly typically synoptic.

1.1. *Teras*

The Greek word τέρας designates an awe-inspiring or terrifying manifestation of supernatural power, usually something monstrous: "portent", "prodigy". In the LXX the word is used more than 20 times together with σημεῖον ("sign") in the cliché "signs and portents" (σημεῖα καὶ τέρατα, corresponding to the Hebrew אותות ומופתים), in most cases to designate the remarkable happenings conjured up by Moses and Aaron at the time of the Exodus from Egypt. What happened then was both terrifying and designed to legitimate the fact that they were sent by God (Ex 3—11). The cliché could also be used in a more colourless sense.

In the New Testament τέρατα occurs 16 times, always in the plural and only in combination with σημεῖα: "signs and portents" or "portents and signs". In one place (Acts 2:19), τέρατα stands alone, but there we have σημεῖα on the next line, in a *parallelismus membrorum*.

We also meet the expression in the synoptic gospels. In the eschatological discourse Jesus warns of false prophets and false Christs who will arise in the future to lead many astray with "signs and portents" (Mk 13:22, Mt 24:24; cf. 2 Thess 2:9). In a similar context of themes, together with "signs" Luke has φόβητρα, "terrible things", instead of τέρατα (21:11).

The awe-inspiring omina and portents which according to the synoptic tradition appear at the time of Jesus' death (Mk 15:33, 38, Mt 27:45,

---

[1] As to the terminology, see the pertinent words in G. Kittel's *Wörterbuch*, and further R. C. Trench, *Synonyms of the New Testament*⁹, Grand Rapids 1976, 339—344, C. F. D. Moule, The Vocabulary of Miracle, in idem (ed.), *Miracles* (Intr.: 2), 235—238, S. V. McCasland, Signs and Wonders, *Journ. of Bibl. Lit.* 46 (1957), 149—152.

51—54, Lk 23:44—48) could well have been designated τέρατα[2] but none of the evangelists needs any summarizing term in this connection.

As for the mighty acts of *Jesus*, in the synoptic gospels they are naturally enough not designated as "portents", but neither are they called "signs and portents". John only touches on this terminology in one place (4:48), where Jesus rebukes the people for not wanting to believe without seeing "signs and portents". There is, however, one place in the New Testament where the cliché "signs and portents" is used of the miracles of *Jesus*: Acts 2:22. Here it is said — in a discourse of Peter — that Jesus was a man "attested to you by God with mighty acts and portents and signs which God did through him in your midst . . ." It seems as if Luke is here portraying Jesus as having been sent by God in analogy to the apostles. Their ministry is presented as being accompanied by "signs and portents" which God does for them and through them as a legitimation of their ministry. This idea is found in Acts (2:43, 4:30, 5:12, 14:3 and 15:12; the last two concern Paul and Barnabas[3])[4] and also in the writings of Paul (Rom 15:19, 2 Cor 12:12), and then again in the letter to the Hebrews (2:4). As a description of the acts of *Jesus*, however, the formulation in Acts 2:22 is unique in the New Testament.

In the conclusion of this section (1.5.), we shall reflect upon why the various terms are used or not used.

1.2. *Sēmeion*

As we have already suggested, the word σημεῖον ("sign") was within the evangelists' reach. It could be found in the Old Testament scriptures, it occurs some 150 times in the LXX (most nearly equivalent to the Hebrew אות). It could be found in the tradition of exposition. And if

---

[2] Or σημεῖα καὶ τέρατα. McCasland points out that Josephus (Bell. VI. 288—309) calls a number of similar events in connection with the fall of Jerusalem "signs and portents", *Signs*, 151. For comparisons with (a) the general Hellenistic usage of language, (b) the terminology in Philo and Josephus, see G. Delling's instructive articles in *Studien zum Neuen Testament und zum hellenistischen Judentum*, Berlin 1970, 53—159. See also O. Betz, Das Problem des Wunders bei Flavius Josephus im Vergleich zum Wunderproblem bei den Rabbinen und im Johannesevangelium, in *Josephus-Studien (Festschrift in honour of O. Michel)*, Göttingen 1974, 23—44. On Hellenistic miracle stories, cf. R. Reitzenstein, *Hellenistische Wundererzählungen*, Leipzig 1906, O. Weinreich, *Antike Heilungswunder, Untersuchungen zum Wunderglauben der Griechen und Römer*, Giessen 1909, R. M. Grant, *Miracle and Natural Law in Graeco-Roman and Early Christian Thought*, Amsterdam 1952, G. Delling, *Antike Wundertexte*[2], Berlin 1960. For more recent literature, see A. George, Miracles dans le monde hellénistique, in Léon-Dufour, *Miracles* (Intr.: 2), 95—108. See also below.

[3] Luke does not consider Paul and Barnabas as being *apostles*; the usage in Acts 14:4, 14 is exceptional. On "the signs of an apostle", see my remarks in Die Boten Gottes und die Apostel Christi, *Svensk Exeg. Årsbok* 27 (1962), 105—116.

[4] Cf. also 6:8 (about Stephen) and 7:36 (about Moses).

we look at the early Christian material we can note that in Johannine circles there was no hesitation in making the word "sign" one of the two main designations for the miracles of Jesus; the other is ἔργον ("work" = מעשה). The synoptists, on the other hand, form a marked contrast.

In fact, both the word and the thing occur in synoptic texts. In the infancy narrative of Luke we have an example of a heavenly messenger giving a "sign" (a sign of recognition and legitimation). He does this on his own initiative: the angel gives such a sign to the shepherds (2:12; cf. 2:16, 20). Zechariah's question to the angel (1:18) is in reality a request for a sign, even if the actual word is not used. Typically enough, the demand is charged as showing unbelief and is punished (1:20).

As we have already mentioned, Jesus prophesies in the eschatological discourse that in the last days false prophets and false Christs will lead people astray with "signs and portents" (Mk 13:22, Mt 24:24), and intimates that before the end of the age there will be terrible things and "great signs from heaven" (Lk 21:11). In this connection the disciples beg to know "what will be the sign when this is about to take place", meaning chiefly the destruction of Jerusalem (Mk 13:4, Lk 21:7). In the Matthean version the question is mainly concerned with "the sign of your coming and of the close of the age" (24:3). This plea results in a discourse from Jesus, where he says among other things, "then will appear the sign of the Son of man in heaven" (Mt 24:30), without any further disclosure as to the nature of this sign.

In the passion narrative, Luke tells how Herod was hoping to see some sign from Jesus, though in vain (23:8). It is possible that in this place Luke is using the term "sign" in the sense of "mighty act",[5] but it is more probable that we have here a variation on the theme of "demanding signs".

Apart from this *possible* exception, the mighty acts of Jesus are in no place in the synoptic gospels designated expressly as "signs". The word σημεῖον appears to have lain under a taboo, in this tradition, and was not to be used of the mighty acts which *Jesus* did during his public ministry in Israel. The explanation of this is not hard to find. One tradition, preserved both in the Marcan material and in the so-called Q material, and reflected in the Gospel of John (Mk 8:11—12, Mt 12:38—39, 16:1—4, Lk 11:16, 29; cf. Jn 2:18—22, 4:48, 6:30) relates that a sign was demanded of Jesus by his adversaries the Pharisees but that he firmly rejected this demand. According to one version — that of Mark — his refusal in this instance was absolute and general (Mk 8:12); according to another version — the so-called Q tradition — although he rejected

---

[5] Luke's miracle terminology seems to be somewhat more vague than that of the other synoptics. On the miracles in Luke, cf. most recently U. Busse, *Die Wunder des Propheten Jesus. Die Rezeption, Komposition und Interpretation der Wundertradition im Evangelium des Lukas*, Stuttgart 1977 (lit.).

the demand he did hold out the prospect of a mysterious future sign, "the sign of Jonah" (Lk 11:29, Mt 16:4, and also included in 12:39).[6]

It seems certain that it is this very tradition which precluded the possibility of the designation "sign" being a term useable for the mighty acts of Jesus in the synoptic gospels. What is the suggestion? As opposed to the usual interpretations that the Pharisees' demand was for either a specially great sign or a sign of an obviously heavenly character ("from heaven"), Olof Linton has with good reason claimed that we are here dealing with a clearly delimited form of sign — a sign which does not in itself need to be great or miraculous[7] but which is stated ("given") in advance and which then appears, all in order to confirm that one who has been sent by God really is genuine: a legitimating sign.[8] The synoptic tradition thus informs us that Jesus refused to legitimate himself in this way. And the use of language in the synoptic gospels shows that those writing within this tradition felt that they were not free to interpret the mighty acts of Jesus as legitimating "signs".

It is interesting, however, to note three points. 1. In the Matthean adaptation of the tradition concerning the Pharisees' demand for a sign, the death and resurrection of Jesus are considered as a sign. For Luke, "the sign of Jonah" seems to be the same as Jesus himself, but for Matthew "the sign of Jonah" is the death and resurrection of Jesus.[9] This sign is clearly stated in advance, even for the adversaries ("some of the scribes and Pharisees", 12:38—40); according to Matthew the high priests and Pharisees have also clearly understood the matter (27:62—66). But they reject it (*loc. cit.*), and when they learn that the sign has been shown they harden their hearts against it (28:2—4, 11—15). Thus the category "sign" has been approved here, not indeed for the mighty acts of Jesus, but for his death and resurrection.

2. In the tradition of how Jesus heals a paralytic, there is one element — probably a secondary interpretation, even if included at a very early stage — in which this healing is seen as a demonstration of the power of Jesus to forgive sins (Mk 2:6—10, Mt 9:3—6a, Lk 5:21—24a). Here the term "sign" is not used, but there is no doubt that this healing is

---

[6] Cf. also John 2:18—22.
[7] Cf. Lk 2:12! In this particular case, however, the adversaries clearly ask for a *miraculous* sign ("from heaven").
[8] O. Linton, The Demand for a Sign from Heaven(Mk 8, 11—12 and Parallels), *Studia Theol.* 19 (1965), 112—129.
[9] I am not sure that J. M. Hull is right when he maintains that in Luke the exorcisms of Jesus are interpreted as "signs", *Hellenistic Magic and the Synoptic Tradition*, London 1974, 117—118. — For the problem in general, see O. Glombitza, Das Zeichen des Jona, *New Test. Stud.* 8 (1961—62), 359—366, A. Vögtle, *Das Evangelium und die Evangelien*, Düsseldorf 1971, 103—136, R. A. Edwards, *The Sign of Jonah in the Theology of the Evangelists and Q*, London 1971, Theissen, *Wundergeschichten* (Intr.: 2), 287—297.

being presented as a sort of sign confirming the claim of Jesus (and of the church) to be able to *forgive sins*. Thus here the "sign" category has *anonymously* been given a place in the synoptic tradition of Jesus' mighty acts (cf. 5.3.2. below).

3. We meet the same phenomenon in another pericope as well: in the controversy dialogue (*Streitgespräch*) concerning the man with the withered hand (Mk 3:1—6, Mt 12:9—14, Lk 6:6—11). The controversy here is about whether it is permissible (according to the will of God) to heal on the sabbath. Jesus declares that it is, and ostentatiously heals the man. In this case the miracle, which has the character of a "norm miracle" (*Normenwunder*),[10] is in actual fact a kind of sign legitimating the message and practice of Jesus on this point, even if the actual term "sign" is absent (cf. 5.3.3. below).

These examples show that within the synoptic tradition it was possible to narrate that with "signs" Jesus had confirmed his authority to forgive sins and his right to heal on the sabbath. In principle, however, it is clear that the mighty acts of Jesus were not considered as legitimating "signs".

1.3. *Thaumasion, paradoxon, endoxon, ergon*

The Greek word most nearly equivalent to our "miracle" (from Lat. *miraculum*) is θαῦμα. In the New Testament it is not used about the mighty acts of Jesus at all. The synonymous term θαυμάσιον ("marvel") is only used in a single place (Mt 21:15, an editorial item). From this, however, one cannot draw the conclusion that the acts of Jesus coalesced with what customarily happened in "a biblical world, full of miracles". Matthew at the very least notes that the mighty acts of Jesus were of an extraordinary nature and aroused the attention and considerable wonder of the people. The crowds marvel (θαυμάζειν) and glorify the God of Israel when they see how Jesus heals sick people (15:31). They marvel when he heals a dumb demoniac and state that nothing like this has ever been seen in Israel (9:33). They are beside themselves with amazement (ἐξίστασθαι) when he heals a blind and dumb demoniac and wonder if he is not the Son of David (12:23). They are afraid (φοβεῖσθαι) when Jesus heals a paralytic, and glorify God, who has given such authority to men (9:1—8). The miracle of the calming of the storm causes "the men" to marvel (8:27), and the disciples marvel that the fig tree withers at once when Jesus curses it (21:20).

The passages quoted show very clearly that Matthew considers the mighty acts of Jesus as *miracles in the sense of extraordinary, sensational events*. It is also clear, however, that this aspect is not so important for him that the term θαυμάσιον (פלא, ונפלאות) becomes a favourite, often used

---

[10] On the *Normenwunder*, see Theissen, *Wundergeschichten*, 114—120.

term for the mighty acts of Jesus. Another aspect is more important for him than the miracle aspect.[11]

It should, perhaps, be mentioned that in one case Luke has the partially synonymous term παράδοξον ("a surprising thing, contrary to expectation",[12] 5:26) and in another place the term ἔνδοξον ("glorious work", 13:17). The use of these words, too, is exceptional.

In one place in the Gospel of Matthew (11:2) we find the summarizing expression τὰ ἔργα τοῦ Χριστοῦ ("the works of the Christ"). Since the surprising point is not the term ἔργον ("work") but the fact that "Christ" is used here and not "Jesus", we hardly need comment on the matter in the present context (see instead 2.3.5.2. below).

1.4. *Dynamis*

The main summarizing designation of the miracles of Jesus used by the synoptists is δύναμις, "manifestation of power", "mighty act". The Hebrew equivalent is גבורה. The term δύναμις does not occur at all in the Johannine scriptures, not in *any* sense. As a designation of Jesus' miracles — worked by himself or "in his name" — the term is used three times in Mark (6:2, 5, 9:39), twice in Luke (10:13, 19:37) and six times in Matthew (7:22, 11:20, 21, 23, 13:54, 58). Only once is the term in the singular (Mk 6:5), otherwise in the plural. This is natural as it is a question of summarizing statements.

For the positive use of the term for the miracles of Jesus it was certainly of great importance that it occurred in pronouncements of Jesus handed down by tradition. Within early Christianity, therefore, it counted as a term which Jesus himself had used of his mighty works (in Aramaic גבורתא).

The tradition of Jesus' words of chastisement concerning Chorazin, Bethsaida and Capernaum (Mt 11:20—24, Lk 10:12—15) belongs to the Q *material*: there are cries of woe because these cities have not repented despite the many "mighty acts" (δυνάμεις) that have been done in them. (The passive construction is probably not a so-called *passivum divinum* but a natural construction, since the predicate must serve two different agents.) In Matthew the expression "mighty acts" has also been taken up in the introductory editorial statement (v. 20). Verse 23 appears to be the result of restoration work, designed to render the pronouncement over Capernaum symmetrical with the one over Chorazin and Bethsaida. The occurrence of the term in this verse is probably secondary (see further 5.2.2. below).

The tradition of Jesus' visit to his home town of Nazareth (Mk 6:1—6, Mt 13:54—58; cf. Lk 4:16—30) belongs to the *Marcan material*. The

---

[11] Cf. Moule, *Miracles*, 235—238.
[12] The phrase stems from Moule, *Miracles*, 237.

reaction of the inhabitants to Jesus' teaching and therapeutic ministry is described as unfavourable: they are astonished both at his "wisdom" (σοφία) and at his "mighty acts" (δυνάμεις) and take offence at him. In the concluding editorial framework both evangelists use the expression again: he does not do many "mighty acts" because of their unbelief. Thus we see that the term "mighty acts" is being used here both in the words of the Nazarenes and in the narrative framework, in Mark as well as in Matthew. Luke uses the term in an editorial statement in 19:37 (see further 5.2.1. below).

The fact that "mighty acts" is also used of the miracles worked "in the name of Jesus" can be seen both in Mark in the pericope of the strange exorcist (9:38—42) and in Matthew in the pericope of false charismatic persons (7:21—23).

The picture becomes quite clear. In both the large groups of material (Mark and Q) and in all three synoptists, "mighty acts" is the favourable term for the miracles of Jesus and thus also for the miracles done "in the name of Jesus".[13] The term refers to actions that are greater than what humans can normally carry out and which therefore cause a sensation and provide a challenge to react — favourably or unfavourably.

1.5. *Concluding remarks*

The survey we have sketched here has given us a preliminary picture of how the synoptics present the miracles of Jesus. The term τέρας was not appropriate: the acts of Jesus were not frightening "portents". Neither was σημεῖον the right word: a tradition was being preserved which showed that Jesus had refused to legitimate himself with the aid of "signs", and his miracles were not interpreted in that way either. The cliché σημεῖα καὶ τέρατα directed the thoughts primarily to the "signs and portents" brought about by Moses and Aaron in Egypt. Jesus' miracles — and this deserves to be emphasized — had little in common with these events. The latter were, after all, of a most frequently destructive character and were brought about for purposes of legitimation; in neither of these respects did they resemble the miracles of Jesus.[14] Neither was the cliché appropriate in a more colourless form: early Christianity did not conceive of Jesus as a prophet whose verbal preaching is merely *accompanied by* or *framed by* "signs and portents" intended to give it a numinous nimbus. The healings and the casting out of demons were — as we shall see — something that

---

[13] For Paul's use of the term δύναμις, in the meaning of "mighty act", see especially Rom 15:19, 2 Cor 12:12, Gal 3:5, I Thess 1:5, and cf. A. Fridrichsen, *Le problème du miracle dans le christianisme primitif*, Strasbourg & Paris 1925, 34—35, Eng. transl.: *The Problem of Miracle in Primitive Christianity*, Minneapolis 1972, 56—57.

[14] On the other hand, the miracles of Jesus show, as we know, many similarities with the saving miracles during the desert wandering.

Jesus *did himself* and they were apprehended as an important part of his real ministry in Israel.

It is self-evident that the term ἔργα was usable. On the other hand, though, this term had no special profile; its meaning was a very general one: "acts", "works", "deeds". The fact that it plays such a role in the Johannine tradition is to a large extent due to it there becoming the object of comment from Jesus' side.[15]

On isolated occasions in the synoptic tradition we find words that present the works of Jesus as sensational and marvellous. In one place Luke has παράδοξον (and in another place ἔνδοξον). Matthew once has the term θαυμάσιον. This shows that it is in principle legitimate to designate the works of Jesus as "wonders" and "miracles" (in the sense of "works which call forth great astonishment"). A further reason for this is given by the observation that the synoptics so often emphasize that the works of Jesus caused people to be *astonished*, to marvel. It deserves to be repeated, however, that this aspect is not important enough to any of the synoptists for the term θαυμάσιον, "marvel", to become a *standing* designation for Jesus' miracles.

For practical reasons I shall often use the term "miracle" in this book. I wish to emphasize once more, however, that I do not take this in the sense of "an act conflicting with the laws of nature" but only in the sense of "an act arousing great astonishment", "a marvel".

The synoptists' natural designation of the miracles of Jesus was δυνάμεις "manifestations of power", "mighty acts". This term was adequate to designate the remarkable actions that Jesus *did*, and it made it evident that it was a question of manifestations of an authority and power greater than what is normally available to humans.

It is part of the character of the mighty acts as much as that of the marvels and signs and the portents in the biblical tradition that they are ambiguous. They can be given a positive interpretation: behind them stands God; this man has been sent by him. Or they can be given a negative interpretation: behind them stand false gods, demons, the spirits of lies and deception; this man is a false prophet leading the people astray (cf. Ex 7: 8—23, Deut 13: 1—3, Mt 24: 24, Mk 13: 22, 2 Thess 2: 8—12, Rev 13: 11—18, 16: 13—14, 19: 20).[16] It is typical that in the traditions

---

[15] On the miracles in the Johannine material, see *Recueil Lucien Cerfaux*, vol. II, Gembloux 1954, 41—50, R. E. Brown, *The Gospel According to John*, vol. I, New York 1966, 525—532, S. Hofbeck, *Semeion. Der Begriff des "Zeichens" im Johannesevangelium unter Berücksichtigung seiner Vorgeschichte*, Münsterschwarzach 1966, W. Wilkens, *Zeichen und Werke. Ein Beitrag zur Theologie des 4. Evangeliums in der Erzählungs- und Redestoff*, Zürich 1969, W. Nicol, *The Sēmeia in the Fourth Gospel. Tradition and Redaction*, Leiden 1972, B. Noack, *Tegnene i Johannesevangeliet. Tydning og brug af Jesu undere*, Copenhagen 1974.

[16] On the theme of deceptive, demonic miracles, see L. Hartman, Antikrists mirakler. Något om motivets förhistoria i judiska texter, *Rel. och Bibel* 26 (1967), 37—63.

of Jesus' mighty acts opinion is divided on which power stands behind them: God or Beelzebul? For the evangelists the matter is clear: Jesus' *exousia* is from heaven. They take trouble to make the matter clear to their listeners as well, both by giving an account of the acts done by Jesus and by telling how he did them. In what follows we shall study the approach taken by *Matthew*.

2. The summarizing accounts of Jesus' therapeutic activity in Israel

The synoptic gospels contain traditions of Jesus healing some person with a certain sickness, and also traditions of his healing many. It seems to me that these types of information should be considered as equally old, in principle. It is certainly incorrect to regard the summarizing accounts only as secondary summaries of the concrete traditions of the individual cases. So the matter stands in principle; the individual summary may, of course, be secondary — and the individual story may also be secondary, if it comes to that.

In common with the other synoptics, Matthew has a number of items briefly stating what Jesus *did* during his public ministry in Israel. As is the custom with him, Matthew has built upon tradition, but he has adapted it: he has abridged it, widened it, stylised it, restructured it or — sometimes — shaped new items of a similar kind. Evidently he considered the tradition to give him sufficient warrant for everything he is telling his readers, even in those cases where he uses his own formulation. He obviously wished to be a traditionist, but one who interprets and clarifies what he is imparting to the listening community.[1]

The summarizing items are of the greatest interest for understanding how the ministry of Jesus in Israel has been apprehended and presented in the Gospel. I shall therefore give a relatively extensive presentation first of all of the results of my analysis of these items. The task is to make clear what these summaries say within the framework of the Gospel of Matthew after its final editing. I shall give an account of certain general data about the material, the gallery of persons, the healing, the sicknesses and the sites of action, and also make some supplementary comments on the individual items, seen in their context. I am not aiming at completeness.

2.1. *The material*

I include the following items in the category of "summaries":[2]
1. (a) 4:23
   (b) 4:24—25

---

[1] See Held's convincing demonstration, *Matthäus* (Intr.: 4), especially 155—158, 284—287, but also 160, 167, 198, 217, 224, 228.
[2] Cf. Léon-Dufour, *Miracles* (Intr.: 1), 388, and Theissen, *Wundergeschichten* (Intr.: 2),

2. 8: 16(—17)
3. 9: 35(—38)
4. 12: 15—16(—21)
5. 14: 13—14
6. 14: (34—)35—36
7. 15: 29—31
8. 19: 1—2
9. 21: 14(—16).

In this chapter, for practical reasons I shall also devote a certain limited amount of attention to two passages which do not have the character of summaries in the same sense as those above but which still in a general and comprehensive manner treat of Jesus' acts of healing. I shall call them "quasi-summaries":

a. 10: 1, (5—)7—8
b. 11: (2—)4—6.

2.2. *The persons*

As we shall see in the next chapter (3.5.), the following *persons* appear as actors[3] in the synoptic stories of Jesus' mighty acts:

Jesus (J)
one or two sick persons (S)
one or more demons (D)
a sick person's companions or representatives (R)
the disciples (Di)
the adversaries (A)
the crowd (C).

Only one story mentions all seven of them: this is the Marcan version of the pericope of the healing of the epileptic boy (Mk 9: 14—29). In other cases we meet a greater or smaller selection of these persons. Sometimes the sick person's representatives (R) are only mentioned implicitly, usually in the verb form when it is said that "they brought" someone to Jesus.

In the Matthean *summaries* the following persons appear:

1a. 4: 23: J (and the diseases)
1b. 4: 24—25: J R(impl.) S C
2. 8: 16: R(impl.) J S D

205—207. The summarizing item in 11: 1 is an exception: this statement indicates that Jesus' ministry of teaching and preaching to the Jews now ceases; see J. A. Comber, The Verb *Therapeuō* in Matthew's Gospel, *Journ. of Bibl. Lit.* 97 (1978), 431—434.

[3] When identifying the persons ("roles") I follow in the main lines Theissen, *Wundergeschichten*, 53—56. His designations are: Wundertäter, Kranker, Dämon, Begleiter, Menge, Gegner, Jünger.

3. 9:35: J(and the diseases)
4. 12:15: J C/S
5. 14:13—14: J C S
6. 14:35—36: J C/R(impl.) S
7. 15:29—31: J C/R S
8. 19:1—2: J C/S
9. 21:14: S J.

Thus there is a rather sparse gallery of persons in the summary items. The main interest is directed at *Jesus*. In two items (1a and 3) only he and the diseases he heals are named, not the sick people. In the remaining summaries, *Jesus* (J) and the *sick persons* (S) always appear. The *disciples* (Di) do not appear at all; neither do the *adversaries* (A) — leaving aside the fact that summary no. 9 is a prelude to a controversy with them. *Demons* are mentioned[4] in one case (2). The sick persons' *representatives* (R) catch our attention at times, but — with one exception (7) — only implied in the verb in the sentences stating that "they" brought sick people to Jesus (1 b, 2, 6). The *crowds* (C) are important in these items; they appear in six cases and are maybe implied in the rest (except no. 9). In 6 and 7 they are representatives of the sick persons (R), and in 4 and 8 they are identical with the latter (S). In the longest summary (7) they also have a more substantial part to play.[5]

This survey itself shows that the story is about *Jesus* and his relation to *the people and the sick among them*. The concentration is so strong that the narrator has no reason to mention either the disciples or the adversaries.

2.3. The individual summaries

So as not to over-generalize I shall — before continuing my analytical *survey* — comment on each summary in turn, seen in its context. They all have their special traits, and several of them fulfil some special function. I shall confine myself to a few aspects.

2.3.1. The programmatic summaries in 4:23—25 and 9:35

Matthew's first complete[6] summary of Jesus' ministry comes in 4:23—25 and is repeated in partly the same words in 9:35. It is obvious that tra-

---

[4] Πνεύματα (8:16). They are also implied in the term δαιμονιζόμενος in nos. 1 b and 2.
[5] As we will see in 3.5. below, the crowds are mentioned in nine — or maybe only eight — of the fourteen pericopes about individual therapeutic miracles, but they do not belong together with the sick person in a single one of these cases: they do not bring him to Jesus or represent him in any other way. — On ὄχλος/ὄχλοι in Matthew, cf. S. van Tilborg, *The Jewish Leaders in Matthew*, Leiden 1972, 142—165, R. Hummel, *Die Auseinandersetzung zwischen Kirche und Judentum im Matthäusevangelium*², München 1966, 136—139, 144—146, J. D. Kingsbury, *The Parables of Jesus in Matthew 13. A Study in Redaction-Criticism*, London 1969, 24—28.
[6] In 4:17 only the *preaching* of Jesus is mentioned.

ditional material has been used here (cf. for instance Mk 1: 14—15, 21, 28—29, 32—34, 39, 3: 7—8),[7] but it is also quite clear that Matthew's own hand has been at work in these two passages; they are cast in his own typical mould.

Under the hand of Matthew, these summarizing items have been given a precise and generalized content:

And he went about all Galilee, teaching in their synagogues and preaching the gospel of the Reign and healing every disease and every infirmity among the people (4: 23).

When the item comes again in 9: 35, the same words are used to give the same information on what Jesus was doing, but here the introductory words are "And Jesus went about all the cities and villages", and at the end the expression "among the people" is absent.

What is most striking is that in these two items — by far the most important summaries in the whole gospel — Matthew states the actual *programme* of Jesus' active ministry. This consists of *a*. teaching and preaching the Reign (ἡ βασιλεία) and *b*. healing every disease and every infirmity among the people.

In this book we shall not be directly occupied with Jesus' preaching (κηρύσσειν) and teaching (διδάσκειν). It will only be touched upon in passing. It is, however, appropriate at this point to make clear that Matthew does not really make any clear distinction between Jesus' preaching/teaching and his therapeutic activity. They belong together. The Matthean Jesus teaches when healing and heals when teaching. Later on we shall see signs of this. It should also be said that preaching and teaching is a more important aspect of Jesus' activity for Matthew than healing. The healing is meant literally but at the same time it is also a form of preaching/teaching. It is no coincidence that the first statement of Jesus' public ministry in Israel runs as follows: "From that time Jesus began to preach, saying "Repent, for the Reign of Heaven is at hand!" (4: 17). The same condensation and abridgement recurs at the end of the Gospel (28: 18—20). There, the disciples are given the task of making disciples of all nations by "baptizing them, . . . teaching them to observe all that I have commanded you", without any special mention of a commandment to heal. It is obvious in other passages in the Gospel, however — we shall return to this — that healing belonged to the tasks given to the disciples. — In 11: 1 we find a summarizing item stating only that Jesus "went on from there to teach and preach in their cities".

In the following I shall simplify matters and use the word "teaching" as a term meaning both preaching and teaching.[8]

---

[7] Cf. Theissen, *Wundergeschichten*, 205—206.
[8] The verbs κηρύσσειν and διδάσκειν are, of course, not synonyms. As an indication we can mention that the disciples are said to preach but not to *teach* (διδάσκειν) during

Both summaries (4: 23 and 9: 35) state that Jesus heals "every disease and every infirmity". This piece of information is given a concrete form in the continuation of the first summary:

... and they brought him all the sick, those affected with various diseases and pains, demoniacs, epileptics, and paralytics, and he healed them (4: 24).

The tendency to magnify and generalize is striking: *a.* "all Galilee", "all the cities and villages", *b.* "every disease and every infirmity", *c.* "all" who were sick. Here, theology — or shall we say: the grandiose perspective of praise and confession — has clearly gained the upper hand over historical correctness.

One important aspect of these programmatic items is worth emphasizing: Jesus himself takes the *basic* initiative of his actions. He is not called out into Israel by the people, he "begins to preach" his message — he goes out to teach and heal.

We will return to 4: 25 later on (2.6.).

2.3.2. *The summaries with formula quotations*

Matthew has not associated any of his celebrated formula quotations with the story of an individual healing. Two *summaries* on the other hand are expressly linked with quotations from the holy scriptures. The "quasi-summary" in 11: 4—6 contains obvious allusions (see 2.3.5.2. below) as well; cf. also 21: 14 (2.3.4.3. below).

2.3.2.1. *The summary in 8: 16(—17)*

Between the two programmatic summaries in 4: 23—25 and 9: 35 Matthew gives us concrete examples of Jesus' teaching (chaps. 5—7) and his mighty acts (chaps. 8—9). Within the last of these two sections (see further 3.2. below) we find a summarizing item which draws, so to speak, the closing line under the first three miracle stories (8: 1—15):[9]

That evening they brought to him many who were possessed with demons; and he cast out the spirits with a word, and healed all who were sick. This was to fulfil what was spoken by the prophet Isaiah, "He took away our infirmities and removed [10] our diseases" (8: 16—17).

This summary is also found — without the quotation from the scriptures — in Mark (1: 32—34) and Luke (4: 40—41). They both give a more lively narration than Matthew. Comparing the Matthean version with the Marcan one, one also notices that Mark lays the main emphasis on

---

Jesus' public ministry (the first occurrence is 28: 20); cf. J. P. Meier, *Law and History in Matthew's Gospel*, Rome 1976, 95—96. But still I do not find it possible to see a *clear* distinction between the two verbs.

[9] Thus Held, *Matthäus*, 161—162, followed by many.

[10] On βαστάζειν, see L. Rydbeck, *Fachprosa, vermeintliche Volkssprache und Neues Testament*, Uppsala 1967, 161—166, 184.

Jesus' exorcistic actions while Matthew reveals his broader and more general view of Jesus' therapeutic activity in this case as in many other places.[11]

In Matthew this short summary fulfils a definite function: it is to serve as the basis for a formula quotation which is brought in from the prophecies of the Servant of the Lord (Is 53: 4, 11). Only Matthew has this quotation, and he has also adapted it *ad hoc*.[12] The wording is not attested in any other Old Testament textual witness. In the quotation the spotlight is not giving a broad and general sweep over what is now happening in Israel but is directed right at *Jesus' person and ministry*; thus the primary function of the quotation is a Christological one. The prophetic words seem to be usable because Jesus is considered as "the Servant of the Lord". According to Matthew, the prophecy in Is 53 about the "Servant" is fulfilled when Jesus "takes away our infirmities and removes our diseases". Here, the "Servant" is brought in from Isaiah not as a figure who brings about healing for the people by suffering and dying for their sins, but as one who takes away the diseases of the people by healing them. Unlike in Is 53, the Servant is not here in Matthew a weak, beaten person but a strong man who heals. He is not a sick person but a physician.[13] The prophetic words and the evangelist's portrayal of Jesus do, however, coincide on a crucial point: the "Servant" frees the people from disease.

2.3.2.2. *The summary in 12: 15—16(—21)*

In chap. 12 we also find a summary which functions as the basis for a formula quotation:

Jesus, aware of this (that his adversaries had taken their decision to destroy him, 12: 14), withdrew from there. And many followed him, and he healed them all, and ordered them not to make him known. This was to fulfil what was spoken by the prophet Isaiah: "Behold, my Servant whom I have chosen, my beloved with whom my soul is well pleased. I will put my Spirit upon him, and he shall proclaim justice to the Gentiles. He will not wrangle or cry aloud, nor will any one hear his voice in the streets; he will not break a bruised reed or quench a smouldering wick, till he brings justice to victory; and in his name will the Gentiles hope" (12: 15—21).

Matthew alone has this summary. We may assume he has built it with the help of elements in the tradition (see Mk 3: 7, 10, 12; cf. also Lk 6: 17—20), in order to obtain a basis for a formula quotation, which we also find only in Matthew. This quotation bears obvious traces of *ad hoc*

---

[11] See most recently D. C. Duling, The Therapeutic Son of David: An Element in Matthew's Christological Apologetic, *New Test. Stud.* 24 (1977—78), 392—410. I will return to this.
[12] For an analysis of the quotation, see K. Stendahl, *The School of St. Matthew and its Use of the Old Testament*², Lund 1964, 106—107, 200, R. H. Gundry, *The Use of the Old Testament in St. Matthew's Gospel*, Leiden 1967, 109, 229—231.
[13] Cf. Held, *Matthäus*, 246—250.

adaptation.[14] What we have here is Matthean reflections on the way Jesus behaves in Israel.

The statement that Jesus withdrew (ἀναχωρεῖν) from an acute threat is typically Matthean. It is also typical of Matthew to say that Jesus heals "them all". Mark is able to say "many".[15] In Matthew, this passage gives the impression that the crowd consists entirely of sick persons, coming to Jesus to receive from him what they seek: healing.

All this is told as the basis for the quotation from the prophecies on the Servant of the Lord (Is 42: 1—4). The quotation does not concern therapeutic actions. This basic matter has already been substantiated with the previous formula quotation (in 8: 17: Is 53: 4). There are now *a number of details in Jesus' way of forming his ministry* which the evangelist connects with the prophecy.

The quotation is remarkably long. Where a long quotation is concerned one may be left uncertain which elements in it are relevant to the person quoting. In this case, however, it seems that Matthew considers all the elements in the quoted text to agree with Jesus' behaviour. As to the beginning and end of the quotation we are sure. Since Matthew is strictly economical in the length of his quotations, one need not suppose that he has included any irrelevant beginning or end. In addition to this general observation one can also note that both the beginning and the end of this quotation reveal conscious adaptation on the part of Matthew.

Like the quotation in 8: 17, this one is also centrally directed at the person and ministry of Jesus. It is applied to Jesus because it speaks of "my Servant" (ὁ παῖς μου), which for the evangelist must apply to the Messiah. Of the latter it is stated at some length that he is "he whom I have chosen, my beloved with whom my soul is well pleased". These words — which reveal the hand of Matthew — have certainly been chosen to direct the thoughts to the words of the voice from heaven in the baptism and transfiguration stories (3: 17, 17: 5), though in these passages the words are "my Son" (ὁ υἱός μου) and not "my Servant". The words of the prophecy "I will put my Spirit upon him" are now fulfilled; this is obviously the intention of the evangelist (cf. especially 3: 16 and 12: 28). The words that he will not wrangle or cry aloud, and that no-one will hear his voice in the streets, fit in primarily with the theme of Jesus' discretion in his healing — that he forbids those who are healed to make him known (12: 16) — but probably also with the statement that Jesus withdraws (12: 15). It is quite clear that Matthew takes the statement that he will not break a bruised reed or quench a smouldering wick as an allusion to Jesus' compassion on those who are small and lost. Matthew also attaches importance to the words that he will proclaim justice to the Gentiles (12: 18 d), and to the final words "till he brings justice to

---

[14] See Stendahl, *School*, 107—115, 198, Gundry, *Use*, 110—116.
[15] Compare especially Mk 1: 32—33 with Mt 8: 16, and Mk 3: 10 with Mt 12: 15. The observation is old.

victory; and in his name will the Gentiles hope" (12: 20 c—21). This is clear from the fact that Matthew has himself adapted the wording.

It thus appears that Matthew considers all the statements in the long quotation as having been fulfilled by Jesus in his actions and ministry. On many points the evangelist has cast the light of the prophecy over Jesus' therapeutic actions in Israel. The ministry he portrays is that of "my Servant" — of the Messiah. Matthew makes the prophetic words serve as an illumination and as a legitimation of Jesus' ministry (see further 6.5. below).

2.3.3. *The preludes to the feeding stories*

In Matthew, the stories of the two feeding miracles are very similar (14: 13—21 and 15: 29—39); we shall return to these further on (4.4.2.). Here we shall briefly comment on the fact that they each have a prelude consisting of a summary of Jesus' healing.

2.3.3.1. *The introduction to the first feeding story, 14: 13—14*

This summary is also found in Mark (and Luke) in the introduction to the story of how Jesus feeds 5 000 men (Mk 6: 32—44, Lk 9: 10 b—17).

The connection with what has gone before is typical of Matthew. The news that John the Baptist has been beheaded is made the reason for Jesus "withdrawing" to a lonely place apart (14: 13). It is here that the crowds throng to him and that the feeding miracle takes place.

The introduction to the story of the feeding miracle fulfils two functions. The first is to explain how the crowd happens to be in such a precarious situation that immediate large-scale feeding becomes necessary (many people, a lonely place, and little food). The second is to explain what Jesus is *doing* in this lonely place where the crowd has sought him out.

Comparison of the three versions shows how differently the three evangelists shape the picture of Jesus in the lonely place. In Mark we read, "As he landed he saw a great throng, and he had compassion on them, because they were like sheep without a shepherd; and he began to teach them many things" (6: 34). In the corresponding place, Luke says, "and he welcomed them and spoke to them of the Reign of God, and cured (ἰᾶτο) those who had need of healing" (9: 11). What Matthew writes is as follows:

As he went ashore he saw a great throng; and he had compassion on them, and healed (ἐθεράπευσεν) their sick (14: 14).

It seems as if Matthew had access to a double tradition — both the Marcan and the Q material — and made a conflation of the two versions. He himself, however, only emphasizes one side of Jesus' ministry in this connection — that he *healed*.

2.3.3.2. *The introduction to the second feeding story, 15: 29—31*

In Luke we miss the story of the feeding of the 4 000 men. Mark has it (8: 1—10), and immediately before it he tells of how Jesus heals a deaf and almost dumb man (7: 32—37). This concrete miracle story is not in Matthew.

In its place — although more clearly linked to the feeding story — Matthew has a summary which seems to be his own creation. If Matthew had access to Mark — in any form — it was probably the final words of the Marcan miracle story that served as his warrant and inspiration: "And they were astonished beyond measure, saying, 'He has done all things well; he even makes the deaf hear and the dumb speak'" (Mk 7: 37). In Matthew the item reads as follows:

And great crowds came to him, bringing with them the lame, the maimed, the blind, the dumb, and many others, and they put them at his feet, and he healed them, so that the throng wondered, when they saw the dumb speaking, the maimed whole, the lame walking, and the blind seeing; and they glorified the God of Israel (15: 30—31).

In the Matthean composition this episode forms an introduction to the feeding of the 4 000 men. What in Mark is an independent story of an individual case of healing is in Matthew a general summary. It also fulfils the same functions as the parallel summary in 14: 13—14: it both explains why the feeding miracle was necessary, and tells us what Jesus was *doing* during his stay on the mountain.

In this summary too we see that Matthew does not say that Jesus is teaching the crowds but only that he heals their sick. While in 14: 13—14, however, he is taken by surprise by the arrival of the crowds, here in 15: 29—31 it is almost as if he is giving a medical consultation. Jesus sits down on the mountainside to receive those who are seeking his aid.

There is no originality in the list of diseases. It is a question of the lame, the blind, the dumb and the maimed, but the formulation "and many others" expands the range of the statement, and the statement that Jesus heals is, as usual, absolute and general: "and he healed them".

As we have said, the summary is an introduction to the following story. However, it possesses its own narrative value. This is apparent not least from the concluding words: the healings make an impression on the crowd; the people marvel and glorify the God of Israel.

2.3.4. *The remaining summaries*

We can treat the three remaining summaries more briefly.

2.3.4.1. *The summary in 14: (34—)35—36*

Between the pericopes of Jesus walking on the water and settling accounts with the Pharisees on the question of washing hands, both Mark and

Matthew have a summary about Jesus healing sick people at Gennesaret (Mk 6: 53—56, Mt 14: 34—36). The summary is a pericope in its own right with its own narrative value.

The Marcan version is as usual broader and more spirited, the Matthean one brief and taut without losing anything essential in content:

And when the men of that place recognised him, they sent round to all that region and brought to him all that were sick, and besought him that they might only touch the fringe of his garment; and as many as touched it were made well (14: 35—36).

Even in Mark the generalization has been carried to some length, but in Matthew it is even more pronounced: "all" that are sick are brought to Jesus. In this summary something is also said of how the healing was done. The motif of "touching the fringe of Jesus' garment" may originally come from the story of the woman with the hemorrhage — if it was not a standing expression — but is already found in the Marcan version of this summary.

Jesus is here portrayed as a healer, a physician. The picture given, though, represents him as strongly influenced by the needs and expectations of the crowd. Jesus heals because he is asked to do so. To put it rather drastically, one can say that the crowd here "uses Jesus" as a source of health.

2.3.4.2. *The summary in 19: 1—2*

After a discourse of Jesus and before the polemic exchange of words with the Pharisees on the question of divorce, Mark has a summarizing item (10: 1). This is also found in the same place in Matthew:

. . . he went away from Galilee and entered the region of Judea beyond the Jordan; and large crowds followed him, and he healed them there (19: 1—2).

As in 12: 15, this sounds as if the whole crowd were sick and were healed. We shall return later to the statements on where this took place (2.6. below).

2.3.4.3. *The final summary, 21: 14(—17)*

In the pericope on the cleansing of the temple (Mt 21: 10—17, cf. Mk 11: 11, 15—17, Lk 19: 45—46), Matthew alone has an interpolation (vv. 14—15). Here we find a sentence which is normally reckoned among the summaries,

And the blind and the lame came to him in the temple, and he healed them (12: 14),

and also a statement that a crowd of children praised him with the cry "Hosanna to the Son of David!" — two circumstances that arouse the indignation of the chief priests and scribes. Jesus, however, defends himself with a verse from the book of Psalms, "Out of the mouth of babes and sucklings thou hast brought perfect praise" (Ps 8:3, LXX).

The man who has come to the temple area and heals people there is accordingly "the Son of David" (cf. also 12:23). We may assume that what is told is seen against the background of the old statute which according to the scriptures went back to King David (2 Sam 5:8), "The blind and the lame shall not come into the house (temple)". "The Son of David" solves the problem by healing the disablements of those who are excluded so that they may then enter. Matthew here sees prophecies fulfilled, such as those in Is 29:18—19, 35:5—6, 42:6—7, Mic 4:6—7 and Zeph 3:19.[16] I find it interesting to note that the psalm quoted here is one of the Psalms of David, and that the "David" in it is addressing one whom he calls "Lord" (κύριος). The technique of using the scriptures seems to be the same here as in the pericope on the question of the Son of David (22:41—46).

In this final summary Matthew places Jesus' healings in Jerusalem and in the temple area itself. It is only right that Jesus' active therapeutic ministry is concluded at the point which was considered the centre of the land of Israel, and indeed of the world.

2.3.5. *The "quasi-summaries"*

As an appendix we shall include two textual elements which are not summaries but which still contain summarizing statements on the ministry of Jesus, here with the disciples as collaborators. From a form-critical point of view it is a question of sayings of Jesus.

2.3.5.1. *Jesus assigns the disciples their task, 10: 1, (5—)7—8*

The summary in 9:35 does not merely represent the conclusion of the composition in 4:23—9:35: at the same time it also forms the transition to the next section, which treats of the disciples being sent out on their mission, 9:36—10:42. One or two elements in this section require a short commentary on our part.

And he called to him his twelve disciples and gave them authority (ἐξουσία) over unclean spirits, to cast them out, and to heal every disease and every infirmity (10:1).

We may assume that Matthew is following the linguistic usage of the tradition — Mk 3:14—15, 6:7 (cf. Lk 9:1—2) — when he thus makes the power over unclean spirits the prerequisite for all healing and not only for exorcisms. He does not generally ascribe every sickness to demonic powers.

---

[16] I have tried to elucidate the Old Testament and Jewish background to this text in C. H. Martling & S. E. Staxäng (ed.), *Kommentar till evangelieboken, Högmässotexterna*, part 3, Uppsala 1964, 484—486.

Here the disciples are given exactly the task which Jesus himself has. The formulation "to heal every disease and every infirmity (θεραπεύειν πᾶσαν νόσον καὶ πᾶσαν μαλακίαν)" is one we recognize from the programmatic summaries concerning Jesus' own ministry in 4:23 and 9:35. The phrase is found only in these places.

In what follows, Jesus' directives are put forward to these disciples when he sends them out. In several places the formulations exceed the compass of the historical situation portrayed — Matthew has his eye not only on the situation before the Passover but also on that after it. In certain respects, however, he keeps within the basic frame. The disciples, for instance, are commissioned not to go to the Samaritans and Gentiles but only to "the lost sheep of the house of Israel". After the Passover this limitation is revoked (28:18—20).[17] The disciples' task is formulated as follows:

And preach as you go, saying, "The Reign of Heaven is at hand". Heal the sick, raise the dead, cleanse lepers, cast out demons... (10:7—8).

For the disciples as well, the main tasks are two — to preach and to heal. This latter task, however, is concretized and clarified in Matthew in a way quite unlike the accounts of Mark and Luke (cf. Mk 3:14—15, 6:7, Lk 9:2). It is obvious that these specifications ("raise the dead, cleanse lepers, cast out demons") have been made against the background of what has been said before about the ministry of Jesus (cf. e.g. 8:1—4, 28—34, 9:18—19, 23—26). In this way it becomes very clear that the disciples are sent out in order to do exactly what Jesus has to do (if we disregard the difference that their preaching, κηρύσσειν, is not yet called teaching, διδάσκειν, cf. 28:20). The fact that it is *Jesus* who gives them the "authority", the *exousia*, and sends them out, means that they are acting in his name.

2.3.5.2. *Jesus' answer to John, 11: (2—)4—6*

This pericope is also found in Luke (7:18—23). Matthew is, as usual, briefer, if we except the actual pronouncement of Jesus in the text.

The introduction is surprising on one point: "Now when John heard in prison about the works of the Christ..." In narrative text, Matthew usually calls the main personage of the Gospel quite simply Jesus. Why does he here write not "the works of Jesus" but "the works of the Christ" (according to the best manuscripts)? The question becomes especially relevant if one adds the observation that the Messiahship of Jesus has not yet been clearly apprehended even by the disciples; this does not happen until 14:33 and 16:16. The answer is probably that in this place Matthew

---

[17] Cf. Joach. Jeremias, *Jesu Verheissung für die Völker*, Stuttgart 1956, and W. Trilling, *Das wahre Israel. Studien zur Theologie des Matthäus-Evangeliums*³, München 1964, 99—105, 124—142.

is not exclusively thinking of the works of *Jesus* but of the Messianic works which Jesus *and his disciples* do. The context — the link with what goes before — makes this likely.[18]

To the question of whether he is "the Coming One" Jesus answers:

> Go and tell John what you hear and see: the blind receive their sight and the lame walk, lepers are cleansed and the deaf hear, and the dead are raised up, and the poor have good news preached to them. And blessed is he who takes no offence at me (11: 4—6).

Jesus' answer places himself in the centre: it is a question of not taking offence at him. The perspective, however, is what eyes and ears that witness the works of Jesus (and his representatives) can apprehend. As usual, there are two main points: healing and preaching. Here, the preaching of the gospel (εὐαγγελίζεσθαι) is mentioned in second place.

The elements of this list of miracles that happen re-echo what has already been told of Jesus' healings. There have been, among others, blind people (9: 27—31), lame people (8: 5—13, 9: 1—8), a leper (8: 1—4), a deaf and dumb man (9: 32—34), and a dead person (9: 18—19, 23—24). According to 10: 7—8, the tasks of Jesus have also been entrusted to the twelve. In that text, the casting out of demons was one of the specifications made. This is not mentioned here.

The wording of the list of marvellous things now taking place is intended to carry the thoughts back to the prophecies of the time of salvation to come and the figure of the Saviour, especially in Is 35: 4—6, 26: 19, 29: 18—19, 42: 18 and 61: 1—2. As for the cleansing of lepers and the raising of the dead, the Elijah and Elisha texts probably also roused expectations for the future: concerning lepers, see 2 Kings 5: 1—14, and concerning raising from the dead see 1 Kings 17: 17—24 and 2 Kings 4: 18—37.[19]

Jesus' answer to John the Baptist is not an explicit "Yes". Matthew, though, certainly conceives this as clear enough all the same. When the acts of Jesus and his apostles are given in a wording that so clearly carries the thoughts back to the many prophecies and expectations of the coming time of salvation and its central figure, the answer must surely be unambiguous for anyone who has "eyes to see with and ears to hear with".

2.4. *Jesus' therapeutic actions*

We can now continue with our *general* questions. What is Jesus *doing* in these items? As we have seen, it is said with highly wrought clarity in

---

[18] Thus Held, *Matthäus*, 239—240.
[19] On the Old Testament background to the miracles in the gospels, cf. e.g. O. Betz & W. Grimm, *Wesen und Wirklichkeit der Wunder Jesu*, Frankfurt am Main, Bern & Las Vegas 1977, H. Riesenfeld, De fientliga andarna (Mk 9: 14—29), *Svensk Exeg. Årsbok* 22—23 (1957—58), 64—74, Moule, *Miracles* (Intr.: 2), 43—79 (J. P. Ross, B. Lindars), Léon-Dufour, *Miracles*, 45—58 (M. Carrez).

the two programmatic summaries (4:23, 9:35) that he devotes himself to two activities: teaching and healing.[20] In the remaining summaries — and I do not include 11:1 here — only one side of this ministry is brought out: the therapeutic activity. The field of vision includes neither the teaching nor any other types of mighty acts. According to the summaries Jesus goes to the crowds to heal them and they come to him in search of healing.

The healing is portrayed concisely and in standard phrases. In one case (14:35—36), the evangelist briefly suggests how it might happen: the sick persons beg to be allowed to "touch the fringe of his garment" and receive aid (διασώζεσθαι) in this fashion. In one summary (8:16) there is also the formulation that he cast out (ἐκβάλλειν) the spirits "with a word (λόγῳ)". But in the other summaries we learn nothing about *how* the healing took place. In them the evangelist uses the summarizing verb θεραπεύειν, "to heal". In 4:23 and 9:35 the present participle of this verb is used. In all six remaining cases the narrator states simply and straight out in the aorist that "he healed (ἐθεράπευσεν)[21] them". This is stylized historiography.

In the pericopes of the individual healings it is typical that Jesus heals when asked to (see 3.7. below). The summary items are as a rule so concise that it is not clearly stated whether Jesus takes the initiative or whether he is asked. In one case, however — in indirect speech — we hear the plea for healing (14:35—36). An initiative on the part of the supplicants may plausibly be said to be implied also in the statement that the sick come to him (21:14) or are brought to him (4:24—25, 8:16—17, 14:13—14, 14:35—36, 15:29—31) and are healed, and this is probably also true of the statements that crowds follow him and he heals them (12:15—21, 19:1—2); see 3.7. below. Jesus' *fundamental* initiative finds expression in the programmatic items in 4:23 and 9:35.

Mark has a general tendency to see diseases as caused by evil spirits and Jesus as an exorcist. This view is also found in certain traditional elements in Matthew (most clearly in 10:1), but the predominant tendency in the first Gospel is to see possession as a sickness by the side of other diseases (e.g. 8:16) and to view the casting out of demons as a form of healing. The verb θεραπεύειν, "to heal", is used not only of the healing of "ordinary" diseases mentioned along with the casting out of demons (8:16; 10:8), but also as a comprehensive term covering exorcistic therapy as well (unambiguously in 4:24, quite clearly also in 4:23 and 9:35, and probably in 12:15, 14:14 and 19:2 as well). Possession, incidentally, is only directly mentioned in 4:24 and 8:16, and the casting out of

---

[20] Or, to be precise, preaching/teaching and healing/exorcism. Cf. above.
[21] For the use of this verb in Matthew, cf. Comber, *The Verb Therapeuō*.

demons only in the latter place. The Matthean Jesus is a therapeutic Messiah, not to any great degree an exorcistic one.[22]

2.5. The diseases

What diseases does Jesus heal according to these summaries? We find (1) a number of general disease designations (I put those which occur in the "quasi-summaries" within square brackets): ἄρρωστος, 14:14, ἀσθένεια, 8:17 (quotation), [ἀσθενεῖν, 10:8], βάσανος, 4:24, κακῶς ἔχων, 4:24, 8:16, 14:35, μαλακία, 4:23, 9:35, [10:1], νόσος, 4:23, 24, 8:17 (quotation), 9:35, [10:1], συνέχεσθαι, 4:24. [Here I also mention νεκρός, "dead", 10:8, 11:5.]

We also find (2) a number of more specific terms: κυλλός, "maimed", 15:30, 31, κωφός, "dumb", [11:5], 15:30, 31, [λεπρός, "leper", 10:8, 11:5] παραλυτικός, "paralytic", 4:24, σεληνιαζόμενος, "epileptic (demoniac)", 4:24, τυφλός, "blind", [11:5], 15:30, 31, 21:14, χωλός, "lame", [11:5], 15:30, 31, 21:14.

As for possession, Matthew uses in the summaries (3) the following designations: [δαιμόνιον 10:8], δαιμονιζόμενος, "demoniac", 4:24, 8:16, πνεῦμα, "spirit" 8:16 [π. ἀκάθαρτον, "unclean spirit", 10:1], σεληνιαζόμενος (cf. above), 4:24.

Concerning those diseases specified more exactly (2) one may observe that Matthew never names a disease in the summaries if he has no example of it in the pericopes of the individual healings. Κυλλός ("maimed") is an exception, but the term does not seem to be far removed from χωλός ("lame"; cf. 18:8) and παραλυτικός. Clearly, Matthew needed a warrant in the tradition for his statements that Jesus healed people with a certain specific disease. This does not mean that he meets our demands of historical exactitude. He has a strong tendency to generalize, using general disease designations (1) and writing that Jesus healed "every" disease and "all" who were sick. Mark does not generalize in the same manner. If one puts all the Matthean summaries together one almost gains the impression that Jesus put an end to ill-health in Israel, in any case in Galilee.

2.6. The places

Matthew is not uninterested in the question of *where* the Messianic events take place. He is careful, for example, to find prophecies showing that the story of Jesus is played out in places indicated by the holy scriptures. I am thinking especially of chaps. 2 and 4.[23] In the latter we find the important item telling us that Jesus' ministry in *Galilee* had been foretold

---

[22] See note 11 above, and cf. 6:12 and 6:14 below.
[23] See K. Stendahl, Quis et Unde? An Analysis of Matthew 1—2, in *Judentum — Urchristentum — Kirche* (Festschrift in honour of Joach. Jeremias), Berlin 1964, 94—105.

by the prophet Isaiah (9:1—2): the great "light" is to appear to "the land of Zebulun and the land of Naphtali, toward the sea, across the Jordan, Galilee of the Gentiles" (Mt 4:15—16). What do the summaries have to say?

The evangelist is particularly concerned to emphasize Jesus' association with Galilee. Jesus spoke and healed in "all Galilee", in "all the cities and villages" there (4:23, 9:35). But since his fame spread throughout all Syria people were drawn to him from other directions as well. Thus all the Jewish areas on both sides of the Jordan were represented in the crowds around him. "And great crowds followed him from Galilee and the Decapolis and Jerusalem and Judea and from beyond the Jordan" (4:25).

When it is said (4:23) that Jesus healed every disease and every infirmity "among the people (ἐν τῷ λαῷ)" this means that he devoted himself to the *Jewish* population.[24] It is certainly no coincidence that Matthew, unlike Mark (3:7—8), omits Tyre and Sidon from his enumeration. A mention of these cities would not have been understood as an allusion to Jews. In the region of the Decapolis, on the other hand, a sufficient number of Jews lived for it to be mentioned as well. Like Mark, Matthew does not mention Samaria, and this is quite certainly intentional. In 15:24, Jesus expressly limits his earthly ministry to "the lost sheep of the house of Israel" and in 10:5—6 we see that Samaria and the Gentile regions are thereby excluded. We may also observe that Matthew mentions neither Samaria nor the Samaritans anywhere in his Gospel except in the pronouncement that the disciples are not to go there (10:5). What Matthew portrays is Jesus' ministry *in Israel*. The time of the Gentiles (cf. 24:14, 25:31—32, 26:13, 28:16—20) has not yet come.

What is stated in the summary in 8:16—17 obviously takes place in Capernaum (cf. 8:5), in Peter's house (8:14), but the location is not underlined in this case. Neither is it said in 12:15—21 explicitly where everything is taking place; to judge by the context it is in Galilee. In 14:34—36 we are on the shore of Gennesaret, in 15:29—31 on a hill (in Galilee). Matthew is not *consistent* in his interest in the location of the events.

In the summary in 19:1—2, however, the evangelist is strikingly aware. He emphasizes, in a somewhat laboured formulation, that Jesus "went away from Galilee and entered the region of Judea beyond the Jordan". This must mean that Jesus came through Perea and crossed the Jordan into Judea.[25] ". . . And large crowds followed him, and he healed them there". The location is emphasized (ἐκεῖ). And yet it is still not clear. Does ἐκεῖ refer to the country beyond the Jordan or to the region of Judea?

---

[24] Thus rightly T. Zahn, *Das Evangelium des Matthäus*³, Leipzig 1910, ad 4:23. Cf. above, note 17.
[25] Zahn, *Evangelium*, ad 19:1. Cf. W. G. Thompson, *Matthew's Advice to a Divided Community, Mt. 17, 22—18, 35*, Rome 1970, 22—25.

Both are possible. In my opinion it seems more plausible to interpret the formulation according to the first alternative. If that is so, Matthew wanted to say that Jesus healed the sick within this Jewish region as well. Otherwise it must be Judea that is stated as the scene of Jesus' collective healings on the way to Jerusalem.

In the last summary we are in the Holy City, in the temple area (21: 14). Here Jesus is healing "the blind and the lame".

If we also consider the fourteen pericopes about the individual healing miracles this means, taken together, that Jesus' therapeutic activity has been associated with all Jewish areas named in the first summary (4: 23—25). The association with the regions on the other side of the Jordan (the Decapolis and Perea) is the loosest. The evangelist is most interested in illuminating Jesus' association with Galilee. The Messiah has visited his people.

2.7. Concluding remarks

Matthew economizes on space. How is it that he has included so many rather similar items about Jesus healing gatherings of sick people?

The repetitions do not advance the account gradually; it is not heightened by them. Apart from the geographical information they contain, the summaries could mostly be interchanged without disturbing the chronology or breaking the chain of events. These items are thus fairly loose tiles with a certain definite colour in the mosaic formed by the Gospel of Matthew.

The repetitions fulfil, however, their function.[26] Since the Gospel contains so much discourse material, the picture of Jesus might easily become that of a *prophet*, attended by certain signs and wonders but with one single main task: to speak. The large number and hyperbolic nature of the items about his healing give a kind of equilibrium to the presentation of the ministry of *the Messiah*.

In the summaries Jesus is not given any exalted titles. There are no verbal exchanges and thus no words of address. And in the narrative text Matthew uses simple designations for the figure he is portraying. He calls him simply Jesus or "he" (αὐτός or implied in the verb).

It is self-evident, however, that Christological aspects are *implied*: all the way along, the Gospel of Matthew is about a man who is given a whole series of Christological designations: the Christ/Messiah, the Son of God, the Servant of God, the Lord, the Son of David and so on. The relation to Christology is sometimes very well revealed in the contexts. A summary may function as the basis for a quotation from the scriptures that treats of "the Servant of the Lord" (8: 16—17, 12: 15—21) or it may

---

[23] For a comparison with the summaries in Mk, see W. Egger, *Frohbotschaft und Lehre. Die Sammelberichte des Wirkens Jesu im Markusevangelium*, Frankfurt am Main 1976.

lead to a quotation from the scriptures about someone whom David calls "Lord" (21: 14—17). In the context to one of the "quasi-summaries" we see that what Jesus and his disciples are doing is called "the works of the Christ" and evokes the question of whether he is "the Coming One" (11: 2—6) and so forth. See further chap. 6 below.

In the Rabbinic tradition there are stories of miraculous healings, but there it is God who heals. Pious men are able — usually through prayer — to secure healing miracles from God.[27] It is characteristic of the synoptic Jesus that he himself heals, in his own name so to speak, with an authority (ἐξουσία) which in some way is one with himself. This is portrayed with simple, clear strokes in the Matthean summaries. The task of Jesus is to teach and heal, and this he does in a miraculous manner.

Matthew quotes the prophecy of how "the Servant of the Lord" is to free his people from their infirmities and diseases (8: 17) and allows Jesus to make allusions to the healing of the coming time of salvation (11: 5). He does not resort to the old divine designation "the healer of Israel"[28] anywhere in his Gospel, but this designation is, so to speak, in the air in 9: 12 and 13: 15, and it would harmonize perfectly with his representation of the Jesus who heals the sick in Galilee, the Decapolis (incidentally), Judea and Jerusalem (and probably also Perea). Jesus acts as *the healer of Israel*, the one who heals the wounds of Israel.[29] In the pericopes of his individual healing miracles we are given a closer insight into his secrets: his incomparable *exousia* and the way in which he exercises it.

---

[27] For a convenient collection of Rabbinic miracle texts, see P. Fiebig, *Rabbinische Wundergeschichten des neutestamentlichen Zeitalters*², Berlin 1933 (Hebr. texts); for translated texts and commentaries, see idem, *Jüdische Wundergeschichten des neutestamentlichen Zeitalters*, Tübingen 1911. See further A. Schlatter, *Das Wunder in der Synagoge*, Gütersloh 1912, I. Heinemann, Die Kontroverse über das Wunder im Judentum der hellenistischen Zeit, in *Jubilee Volume in Honour of Prof. Bernhard Heller*, Budapest 1941, 170—191, L. Sabourin, Hellenistic and Rabbinic "Miracles", *Bibl. Theol. Bull.* 2 (1972), 281—307, E. E. Urbach, *The Sages. Their Concepts and Beliefs*, vol. I, Jerusalem 1975, 75—123, Léon-Dufour, *Miracles*, 73—94 (K. Hruby).
[28] The classical formulation is to be found in Ex 15: 26: "I am the Lord, your healer".
[29] The prophetic picture of Israel as hurt and wounded so that God must heal it, is common especially in Isaiah and Jeremiah; see e.g. Is 1: 4—6, 30: 26, 53: 1—5, 58: 8, Jer 10: 19, 30: 12—17, 33: 4—7. A. von Harnack wrote brilliant pages on the motif "Jesus als Artz" in the Ancient Church, in *Die Mission und Ausbreitung des Christentums in den ersten drei Jahrhunderten*⁴, vol. 2, Leipzig 1924, book 1, chaps. 2—3. I have used the second edition (87—126).

3. The pericopes of Jesus' therapeutic miracles in individual cases

Apart from the summarizing accounts of Jesus' therapeutic activity in Israel — items to which Matthew accords independent narrative and interpretative value — the first evangelist has a number of pericopes of how Jesus heals in individual cases: one or two people who are sick or possessed. I am using expressions such as "therapeutic activity" or "therapeutic stories" as general terms for both healings of disease and exorcisms of demons, and for accounts of both kinds of therapy. The designation "miracle story" is not used here in a technical, form-critical sense but only as a simple, conventional name for a pericope telling of a miracle worked by Jesus, even if the miracle is by no means in the centre of the narrative.

3.1. *The material*

Matthew tells of Jesus healing the following sick people. In the healings I am including the raising from the dead of the ruler's daughter (6):[1]

1. A leper, 8: 1—4 (Mark 1: 40—45, Luke 5: 12—16)
2. A centurion's servant, 8: 5—13 (Luke 7: 1—10)
3. Peter's mother-in-law, 8: 14—15 (Mark 1: 29—31, Luke 4: 38—39)
4. Two demoniacs, 8: 28—34 (Mark 5: 1—20, Luke 8: 26—39)
5. A paralytic, 9: 1—8 (Mark 2: 1—12, Luke 5: 17—21)
6. A ruler's daughter, 9: 18—26 (Mark 5: 21—43, Luke 8: 40—56), which includes a separate independent narrative (7):
7. A woman with a hemorrhage, 9: 20—22 (Mark 5: 25—34, Luke 8: 42 b—48)
8. Two blind men, 9: 27—31
9. A dumb demoniac, 9: 32—34
10. A man with a withered hand, 12: 9—14 (Mark 3: 1—6, Luke 6: 6—11)
11. A blind and dumb demoniac, 12: 22—32 (Mark 3: 20—30, Luke 11: 14—23)
12. The daughter of a Canaanite woman, 15: 21—28 (Mark 7: 24—30)
13. A man's epileptic son, 17: 14—20 (Mark 9: 14—29, Luke 9: 37—43)
14. Two blind men, 20: 29—34 (Mark 10: 46—52, Luke 18: 35—43).

[1] The pericopes about raising from the dead are in neither form nor content similar to the stories about the "nature miracles".

Eleven of the fourteen pericopes belong to what we call the Marcan material, and only one (2) to the Q material. Two of them are found only in Matthew: 8, which is a parallel to 14, and 9, which is a parallel to 11.[2]

Nine of the fourteen cases concern healings of some named disease (1, 2, 3, 5, 6 [raising from the dead], 7, 8, 10, 14); five cases concern exorcisms (4, 9, 11, 12, 13).

3.2. *The collection in chapters 8—9*

The list shows that no less than nine of these fourteen therapeutic miracle accounts are contained in chapters 8 and 9. Matthew has five large discourse compositions in his gospel but only this single large collection of miracles. The remaining five therapeutic narratives are spread out over chapters 12—20.

The collection in chapters 8—9[3] requires a commentary. This composition with its four subdivisions (8:1—17, 8:18—9:17, 9:18—31, 9:32—34)[4] is an important block within the Gospel of Matthew. Commentators usually call this block a miracle cycle or "the ten miracles of Jesus" (including the calming of the storm) or else say that the Jesus who appears in chapters 5—7 as *der Messias des Wortes* (the Messiah of the Word) appears in chapters 8—9 as *der Messias der Tat* (the Messiah of Acts).[5] Such characterizations seem reasonable. These five chapters are preceded by the summary in 4:23—25, where it is said that Jesus (a) taught and preached the gospel of the Reign and (b) healed every disease and every infirmity among the people, and it is followed by a summarizing comment which says the same, partly in the same words (9:35). It is clear that chapters 5—7 and 8—9 should be seen in the light of these framework statements (cf. 2.3.1. above).

C. Burger, however, has correctly pointed out[6] that one must not oversimplify the matter. The summaries before and after (4:23—25, 9:35) are not formulated as an introduction of a "colon" type and a summmarizing conclusion pure and simple. They say that Jesus went *about all*

---

[2] "St. Matthew adds no clear and distinct miracle-story to those narrated by St. Mark (except the Q story of the Centurion's Servant). His additions to the Marcan miracle-narratives are, in Streeter's words, 'parasitic; they stand to Mark as mistletoe to the oak'", A. Richardson, *The Miracle-Stories of the Gospels*[11], London 1975, 105.

[3] Cf. C. Burger, Jesu Taten nach Matthäus 8 und 9, *Zeitschr. für Theol. und Kirche* 70 (1973), 272—287, W. G. Thompson, Reflections on the Composition of Mt 8:1—9:34, *The Cath. Bibl. Quart.* 33 (1971), 365—388, J. D. Kingsbury, Observations on the 'Miracle Chapters' of Matthew 8—9, *ibidem* 40 (1978), 559—573, and Theissen, *Wundergeschichten* (Intr.: 2), 210—211.

[4] Held, *Matthäus* (Intr.: 4), 234—237, followed by many. Cf. R. H. Fuller, *Interpreting the Miracles*[6], London 1974, 77—82.

[5] This very common opinion stems (see Burger, *Jesu Taten*, 272) from J. Schniewind, *Das Evangelium nach Matthäus*, Göttingen 1937, 36 and 103.

[6] Burger, *Jesu Taten*.

Galilee, or *about all the cities and villages* and that he taught *in their synagogues*. Chapters 5—7 only contain, however, *a single extensive discourse* of Jesus, and this is given *up on a mountain*. What is narrated in chapters 8—9, moreover, takes place *in and near Capernaum* and in connection *with a visit to Gadara*, and is not spread out over the whole of Galilee. It is also striking that the material in chapters 8—9 contains other elements as well, apart from therapeutic narratives. It is perhaps not very important that there is here a summary with a quotation from the scriptures (8:16—17), but it surely is significant that we here find two apothegms concerning men who wish to follow Jesus but are given a warning (8:18—20, 21—22), and also the narrative of the calming of the storm (8:23—27), as well as the portrayal of the call of Matthew, followed by a polemical exchange of words with the Pharisees on eating with sinners (9:9—13) and the talk with the disciples of John the Baptist concerning fasting (9:14—17). The material is thus mixed. To this we must add that the miracle narratives have been reworked so that they very much bear the character of instructive dialogue. It is obvious that the evangelist has not had the simple aim of presenting a miracle cycle by itself, of telling of the "ten miracles of Jesus" or of specially representing the Messiah of Acts. He makes no clear distinction between the Messiah of the Word and the Messiah of Acts. In his actions the Messiah teaches and preaches at the same time as healing and driving out demons. Thus he is the Messiah of the Word in chapters 8—9 as well. We shall illuminate this more closely further on.[7]

In this study, however, I shall not make a closer examination of the question of the contexts and the major redactional patterns. This is a deliberate delimitation of the task in hand.

3.3 *The form*

One of the characteristics of the Gospel of Matthew is that the *form* of the presentation has been polished with an unbelievable degree of consciousness and care. A telling example of this is the narrative of the healing of Peter's mother-in-law (8:14—15). B. Olsson[8] has drawn attention to the structure of this pericope in the Greek text:

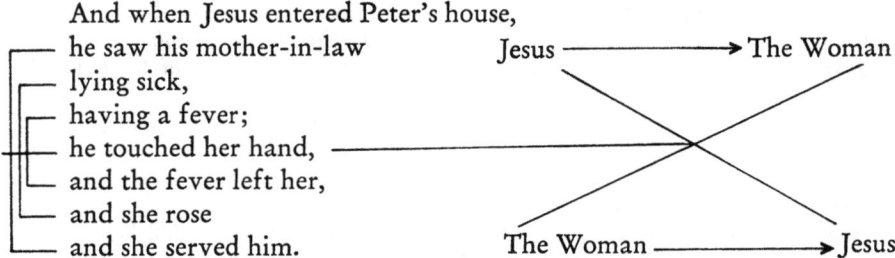

[7] I agree only in part with Burger's own interpretation.
[8] B. Olsson, Att umgås med texter, *Svensk Teol. Kvartalskr.* 52 (1976), 52—53.

There are no spoken exchanges here. The *form* of the pericope, however, emphasizes the universal implications of this singular episode: when Jesus comes to a sick person she is saved through the contact with him and becomes his devotee. To meet the objection that the form of the narrative may be a matter of natural spontaneity, Olsson has rightly referred to the parallels in Mark and Luke (1: 29—31 and 4: 38—39 respectively); this precise design is not found there. It is certainly Matthew who has processed the narrative and given it this strictly executed *inclusio* structure. One may add to this the observation of Joest Smit Sibinga [9] that the two verses of this carefully structured pericope have (in Greek) the same number of words (15) and even the same number of syllables (30). All this, taken together, does not suggest the work of an unreflective narrator. It shows what a high degree of sophistication we can find in the first gospel as regards the *form* of the representation. I shall not present analyses of this type of the 13 remaining pericopes. This example is only given so as to draw attention to the matter.[10] (See also 4.2. below.)

As far as the form of the concrete miracle stories is concerned, H. J. Held has clarified the principles of Matthew's technique in detail and at length in his remarkable study *Matthäus als Interpret der Wundergeschichten*. Conciseness of narrative and description is one of the typical traits of the form of these pericopes. There is only a minimum of vivid detail, incidental circumstances and accessory figures. The actual *narration* normally takes the form of short, standard phrases at the beginning and end of each pericope. The main interest is focussed on the dialogue taking place between Jesus and the person seeking his aid, and especially on the crucial words of Jesus. Matthew stylizes both the plea of the supplicant and the answer of Jesus. In both cases he prefers direct speech to indirect. In this way the pericopes, which in Mark and Luke have the form of animated *Wundergeschichten* ("miracle stories"), have in Matthew almost assumed the form of *Apophthegmata* ("pronouncement stories") — to use the terminology of Bultmann.[11] To this we can add the observation of G. Theissen that the Matthean version of a pericope is generally marked by a simpler and neater structure than the Marcan and Lucan parallels. Matthew has not been content to reproduce mixed, complicated forms of representation as provided by others.[12]

[9] Orally to me.
[10] Prof. J. Smit Sibinga has in a series of articles shown what puzzling figures appear if one counts the syllables in certain early Christian texts, not least in Matthew. See concerning Matthew, Eine literarische Technik im Matthäusevangelium, in M. Didier (ed.), *L'Évangile selon Matthieu. Rédaction et théologie*, Gembloux 1972, 99—105, and: The Structure of the Apocalyptic Discourse, Matthew 24 and 25, *Studia Theol.* 29 (1975), 71—79. It is hard to interpret these observations but I think Prof. Smit Sibinga har here made important discoveries.
[11] Held, *Matthäus*, 229—234. Cf. O. Perels, *Die Wunderüberlieferung der Synoptiker in ihrem Verhältnis zur Wortüberlieferung*, Stuttgart-Berlin 1934.
[12] Theissen, *Wundergeschichten*, 176—178.

3.4. The diseases

The diseases, which are mentioned in our pericopes — with substantives, adjectives or verbs — are designated as follows:

1. General words denoting suffering: βασανίζεσθαι, 8:6, πάσχειν, 17:15. The expressions for dying are ἀποθανεῖν, 9:24, and τελευτᾶν, 9:18.

2. More specific terms: αἱμορροοῦσα, "suffering from a hemorrhage", 9:20, κωφός, "dumb", 9:32, 33, 12:22, λέπρα, "leprosy", 8:3, λεπρός, "leper", 8:2, παραλυτικός, "paralytic", 8:6, 9:2, 6, πυρέσσειν, "have a fever", 8:14, πυρετός, "fever", 8:15, σεληνιάζεσθαι, "be an epileptic (demoniac)", 17:15, τυφλός, "blind", 9:27, 28, 12:22, 20:30, χεῖραν ἔχων ξηράν, "with a withered hand", 12:10.

3. As to possession we find that the evil spirit is called δαίμων in 8:31, and δαιμόνιον in 9:33, 34, [12:24, 27, 28], 17:18. The verb for being possessed (δαιμονίζεσθαι) occurs in 8:28, 33, 9:32, 12:22, 15:22. Σεληνιάζεσθαι (17:15; see above) should also be mentioned.

I am not going to discuss these terms [13] this time. (Cf. 2.5. above.)

3.5. The persons

The persons [14] appearing in the pericopes of the individual cases of healing are the following:

1. The leper, 8:1—4: J C S
2. The centurion's servant, 8:5—13: J R S, also either C or Di
3. Peter's mother-in-law, 8:14—15: J S
4. The two demoniacs, 8:28—34: J S D C
5. The paralytic, 9:1—8: J R S A C
6. The ruler's dead daughter, 9:18—19, 23—26: J R Di C S
7. The woman with a hemorrhage, 9:20—22: J S
8. The two blind men, 9:27—31: J S
9. The dumb demoniac, 9:32—34: J R S C D A
10. The man with a withered hand, 12:9—14: J S A
11. The blind and dumb demoniac, 12:22—32: J S R(impl.) C D A
12. The daughter of the Canaanite woman, 15:21—28: J R S Di
13. The epileptic boy, 17:14—20: J C R S D Di
14. The two blind men, 20:29—34: J C S.

The gallery of figures is richer than in the summaries. The central role is always played by *Jesus* himself (J). This is even true of 13, even though Jesus is here mainly teaching about the disciples' power of healing. Thus the pericopes do not treat by and large of sick people and healing, but

---

[13] For disease designations in other material, see 9:12, 12:43—45, 18:8, 25:36, 39, 43, 44, 26:6. See also note 5:3 below.

[14] For the designations, see 2.2. above.

of *Jesus'* healing and how he does it. Jesus is always introduced first in these narratives. Opposite him there are one or more *supplicants*, in half the cases the sick person or persons (S) and in the remaining half one or more representatives (R) of the sick. It is typical of the latter cases (2, 5, 6, 9, 11, 12, 13) that the narrator is interested in what passes between Jesus and this representative, the fate of the sick person being in the background and merely showing that what Jesus says is true. The sick person or persons are mentioned, however, in all fourteen narratives. In three of them (3, 7, 8) it is only Jesus and they who appear. In one case (10) the sick person is mainly an object of instruction, the dialogue here being between Jesus and his adversaries (A); see 5.3.3. below. Demons (D) are mentioned in four cases (4, 9, 11, 13); they are implied in one (12).

The narrator shows only slight interest in the *supplicants* as such. Nothing is said of their previous history or of how they fared afterwards. They appear suddenly and briefly in the circle of light around Jesus, only to leave it again almost at once.[15]

The *disciples* (Di) appear very seldom in the synoptic narratives of the therapeutic miracles of Jesus. The portrayal concentrates to such an extent on what takes place between Jesus and the supplicants that there is not much interest to spare for the disciples. In Matthew they appear in three of the narratives we are considering here. In no. 6 they are mentioned — dutifully — without being given any other part than to follow Jesus. They have been taken over from tradition. They are found also in the parallels in Mark (5: 21—43) and Luke (8: 40—56), both times in the account of how Jesus raises Jairus' daughter and in the intercalated account of the woman with the hemorrhage as well, and in these versions they have a function. In Matthew they are only retained in the basic narrative (6) and they have no real purpose. In no. 12, the disciples do have a part to play, but it is a negative one — they beg Jesus to send away this "heathen" woman who is seeking his aid. This is a specifically Matthean element, and it is not a mere accident that it has been inserted in this place. The opinion of the disciples corresponds to statements that both Jesus himself and his disciples are to limit themselves to "the lost sheep of the house of Israel" (cf. 2.6. above). The disciples' interference is therefore intended to further emphasize the rule which Jesus is here obliged to violate. In the third case (13), the whole pericope is primarily aimed at answering the question of why the disciples were unable to heal the epileptic boy. This narrative is notable for its focus on the disciples. We shall consider it in the following chapter (4.6.). The expression "those who followed him" in no. 2 can hardly be taken as referring to the disciples as a distinct group (see below).

The *adversaries* (A) are not as a rule integrated in the narratives of how Jesus heals. In Matthew they are mentioned in four cases. In two

---

[15] Cf. R. Bultmann, *Die Geschichte der synoptischen Tradition*[4], Göttingen 1968, 235.

of these, however (9 and 11), they are only mentioned after the short narrative of the healing: it is said in connection with the narrative that the people were enthusiastic whereas the adversaries made an unfavourable interpretation of the healing. As for the remaining two cases (5 and 10), they are mainly polemical exchanges with the adversaries and not primarily proper miracle narratives (see further 5.3. below).

The *crowds* (C) are mentioned in the majority of these narratives, that is, in nine or possibly only eight [16] of the fourteen. As we saw in the previous chapter, the summaries give a fairly uniform picture: the crowds seek Jesus to receive aid for their own part or for their sick (see 2.2. and 2.6.—7. above). In the pericopes of the individual cases the picture is different and more differentiated. Here, the crowd has nothing to do with the sick person, not bringing him to Jesus nor representing him in any other way. Neither does the crowd behave so uniformly as in the summaries.

In five of the fourteen pericopes, the crowd is not mentioned at all (3, 7, 8, 10, 12). One pericope is problematic in this respect: no. 2, where Jesus addresses the generalizing teaching to "those who follow him", which appears to refer to the crowds (already mentioned in 8:1) rather than to the disciples: in any case, it can hardly be the disciples alone who are meant. In two pericopes, the crowds are mentioned in the introduction without being given any function in the actual narrative: great crowds follow him (1), and he comes to the crowd (13).

In four cases, the reaction of the crowd to the miracle is stated: the crowds are afraid and glorify God who has given such *exousia* to men (5), they marvel, saying, "Never was anything like this seen in Israel" (9), they are amazed and say, "Can this be the Son of David?" (11). In the Hellenistic region around Gadara, the reaction of the people is one of rejection: "all the city" comes out to meet Jesus and the people beg him to leave their neighbourhood (4).[17]

In the two remaining pericopes, the people play a part in the course of events itself: the crowd try — probably in well-meant concern for Jesus — to prevent two blind men from troubling the master (14), and they laugh at his words that the ruler's daughter is not dead but sleeping (6).

Thus the crowd is only part of the *background* in these narratives, and it does not always play the same role. It is typical, however, that here as well it is shown as having an open-minded, positive attitude to Jesus, though by no means one of perspicacity and confession (cf. 5.3.1. below). Only in two cases is the crowd reaction negative: in pericopes 6 and 4.

---

[16] Depending upon one's interpretation of "those who followed him" in 8:10.
[17] Concerning the turning away of Jesus, see Theissen, *Wundergeschichten*, 81, 149, 177, 252—253. Cf. R. Pesch, The Marcan Version of the Healing of the Gerasene Demoniac, *The Ecum. Rev.* 23 (1971), 349—376.

In the latter, however, it is not a question of a Jewish crowd but of "all the city", alluding to Hellenistic Gadara. (Cf. 5.2. below.)

The most important observations are that the chief figure in the narratives is always *Jesus*, and that what is narrated is always primarily a question of what takes place between Jesus and the *individual supplicant*, whether the latter is asking aid for himself or for some person close to him. The crowds are always only in the background, the disciples and adversaries only receiving occasional mention.

3.6. *The principal themes of the pericopes: the* exousia *of Jesus and the faith of men*

Our survey of the summaries (chap. 2 above) has shown how Matthew emphasizes the statements that Jesus heals the people — or the sick among the people. The therapeutic activity is brought out as one of the chief aspects of his ministry in Israel. The same accentuation is also seen in the fact that Matthew has included no less than fourteen narratives of how Jesus heals in individual cases.

It is quite clear, however, that Matthew does not give an account of these fourteen cases merely in order to provide concrete examples. The pericopes are intended to serve more specific aims. The evangelist reveals in these narratives the inner secrets of Jesus' activity. Matthew has taken, as it were, X-ray photographs of a number of cases and now gives us a clearer view of what is happening behind appearances.

Even the bare facts of which I have given an account above as regards the form of the pericopes (3.3.) and as far as the dramatis personae are concerned (3.5.), show where the main interest of the evangelist lies. He has put *the relationship between Jesus and the supplicants* under the magnifying glass. He is concerned to show clearly the *exousia* of Jesus and the faith of the supplicants, and what happens when the two meet. Matthew considers that he has understood the inner secrets of Jesus' healing miracles, and he lets both Jesus and the supplicants speak of this explicitly and unmistakably. The most important points in these pericopes are expressed in the *dialogues*.[18]

For Matthew, Jesus is a divine figure — the Messiah, the Son of the living God, possessing an incomparable *exousia*. Nothing is too hard for him. He heals every person and he does it with ease. Matthew has long since ceased finding anything *surprising*, for his own part, in the therapeutic miracles of Jesus. As we have already pointed out, the narrative portions of the pericopes are expressed shortly and in standard phrases. This is not the writing of a narrator who has preserved his own sense of amazement at what he is telling. Both Mark and Luke narrate in a different manner.

---

[18] Held demonstrates this in a convincing way, *Matthäus*, 200—234.

The healing itself is always carried out with majestic supremacy. Jesus does not ask God to heal, far less does he heal in any other name. He heals by himself, and he does this by his mere word and — sometimes — by touching the sick person: by touching him (8:3), by touching or taking her hand (8:15, 9:25) or, in the case of blind men, by touching their eyes (9:29, 20:34). It is foreign to Matthew to mention other means or manipulations as does Mark (7:33, 8:23).[19]

In certain cases the pericope is so concise that there is no hint of Jesus' words or his method of procedure. This applies to the almost parallel narratives in 9:32—34 (that of the dumb demoniac) and 12:22—32 (that of the blind and dumb demoniac), which are both intended to serve as a summary basis for the information that the people show an attitude of open approval of Jesus' actions while the Pharisees reject them and level the Beelzebul accusation. The actual narration is finished off in each of these pericopes in a mere 16 words. All we are allowed to know of the healing is that the evil spirit was driven out, and that Jesus healed the sick man (see further 5.3.1. below).

In the similarly concise narrative of the healing of Peter's mother-in-law (8:14—15), all that is said is that Jesus touched her hand, and in the case of Jairus' daughter (9:18—19, 23—26) that he took her by the hand. In neither case is there any indication of what Jesus said.

In the pericope of the healing of the epileptic boy (17:14—20) it is stated that Jesus spoke severely (ἐπιτιμᾶν) to the demon (or possibly the boy), without his words being quoted.

In the remaining pericopes of individual healings, however, the *words* with which Jesus heals the sick person are explicitly stated. We shall now make a brief account of each case.

What is remarkable about the words uttered by Jesus in the Matthean healing narratives is — as Held has shown — that they are not secret words of power such as ταλιθὰ κοῦμ in Mark 5:41 or ἐφφαθά in Mark 7:34.[20] True, they are powerful words, but they are of a more or less instructional character. The Matthean Jesus is like a teaching physician at a university hospital: as he treats the patient, he explains and reveals what is happening. What he explains, however, is not the disease but the cure: his words cast light upon the healer, the healing and the person healed. And what heals the patient is in most cases these instructional words themselves. The teaching is healing and the healing is teaching.

---

[19] Cf. J. M. Hull, *Hellenistic Magic* (1:9), 133—141. Cf. C. Bonner, Traces of Thaumaturgic Technique in the Miracles, *Harv. Theol. Rev.* 20 (1927), 171—181. In my opinion both J. Kallas (*The Significance of the Synoptic Miracles*, London 1961) and O. Böcher (*Dämonenfurcht und Dämonenabwehr. Ein Beitrag zur Vorgeschichte der christlichen Taufe*, Stuttgart & Berlin 1970) "demonize" the New Testament view of existence too strongly.

[20] Held, Matthäus, 230, 262, 272. On ῥῆσις βαρβαρική in miracle stories, see Bultmann, *Geschichte*, 238, and Theissen, *Wundergeschichten*, 73—74, 96—97, 151—153, 252—253.

In the first of the concrete healing narratives (8: 1—4), a leper says, "Lord, if you will, you can make me clean." Jesus answers, "I will; be clean." What is made clearest here is the *power* (δύνασθαι) of Jesus: he can do what he wishes. His *will*, however (θέλειν), is also emphasized: it is to have pity and to help. He helps in such a way that the person in need receives what he begs for. In this case a leper is healed and made clean.[21]

Within parenthesis we might say that Matthew is obviously concerned to emphasize that Jesus' healings are acts of *mercy* and love. In the summaries in 9: 36 and 14: 14 it is said in a general manner that Jesus has compassion (σπλαγχνίζεσθαι) on the crowds when he sees them or when they come to him. The same expression is used in the narrative of how Jesus heals the two blind men in 20: 34. The motif is also apparent in the supplicants' plea for healing. They plead with Jesus to have mercy (ἐλεεῖν) on them (9: 27, 15: 22, 17: 15, 20: 30—31). This means that his intervention is to be interpreted as an act of mercy and love.[22]

In the pericopes of how Jesus heals the centurion's servant (8: 5—13) and the daughter of the Canaanite woman (15: 21—28) — which show considerable parallelism — the healing itself is placed well in the background. In the foreground is the meeting between a "heathen" supplicant and a Jesus whose earthly ministry is confined to Israel.[23] In both cases the supplicant shows unlimited faith (πίστις, πιστεύειν) in Jesus' power to help: one single word from the mouth of Jesus, one little crumb from the master's table, is all they demand, but it will be enough for their protégés to be healed. Jesus gives in to their undaunted faith and exclaims, "Go; be it done for you as you have believed" and, "O woman, great is your faith! Be it done for you as you desire."

The woman with a hemorrhage (9: 20—22) says to herself, "If I only touch the fringe of his garment, I shall be made well." In Mark the healing also takes place in this impersonal manner (Mark 5: 25—34). In the Matthean version, however, everything is at the conscious, personal level. Jesus perceives what the woman wants and what she believes, and he heals her consciously: "Take heart, daughter; your faith has made you well."

The two blind men who in 9: 27—31 beg Jesus to have mercy on them are asked, "Do you believe (πιστεύειν) that I am able to do this?" When they answer in the affirmative, Jesus heals them with the words "According

---

[21] For a hypothesis of the development of this narrative, see C. H. Cave, The Leper: Mark i. 40—45, *New Test. Stud.* 25 (1978—79), 245—250. Cf. also Pesch, *Jesu ureigne Taten?* (Intr.: 5), 52—113.

[22] See my article *Gottes Sohn* (Intr.: 7), 84—88. Cf. Held, *Matthäus*, 208—211, 245—246, 250—257, Richardson, *Miracle-Stories*, 29—34, and G. Braumann, Jesu Erbarmen nach Matthäus, *Theol. Zeitschr.* 19 (1963), 305—317.

[23] Cf. Jeremias, *Verheissung* (2: 17), 22—33. See also 2.6. and 3.5. above.

to your faith be it done to you." These rejoinders make clear with didactic over-explicitness what power Jesus has and what faith is possessed by the supplicants. In the almost parallel narrative of the two blind men in 20: 29—34 the same thing happens, the difference being that they are asked what they want (θέλειν) Jesus to do for them. When they reply to the question he has pity on them and does what they want. Thus the will of the sick people (to be helped) meets Jesus' will (to help). With varying accentuation, both pericopes say the same thing: faith will be given what it wants by Jesus Christ.

In two cases one may perhaps say that the saying of Jesus is rather a word of power than one of instruction; these two cases are the pericope of the paralytic (9: 1—8) and that of the man with the withered hand (12: 9—14). Even here, though, it is not a question of cryptic formulae (ῥῆσις βαρβαρική). In both narratives — where consideration of the adversaries present plays a part — the words of Jesus are orders to do the impossible. The paralytic is told to rise and walk, the man with the withered hand is told to stretch it out. In neither case is the word faith mentioned. We can hardly be mistaken, however, if we consider that faith is implied here: at the word of Jesus, the sick person is to show that he is well. If one is a paralytic one cannot rise, if one's hand is withered one cannot stretch it out (see further 5.3.2.—3. below). The distance between this and the command to Peter to walk on the water (14: 28—31) is not very great. And in this pericope it is apparent that faith is a prerequisite (cf. 4.3.3., 4.6. below).

The narratives of exorcisms of demons are in a class by themselves; we cannot expect the theme of faith to play a prominent part in them. How does Matthew portray Jesus' exorcisms?

Mark can give an animated and dramatic account of how Jesus contends with demons and disease. In a vivid popular style he is able to give a picture of how tough and hard the fight is: the disease does not yield at once, and the demon flees only after counter-attacking. As examples, we can mention Mark 1: 23—28, 7: 31—37 and 8: 22—26. This way of stating the facts does not agree with either Matthew's taste or his picture of Jesus. In his eyes the Master is high and all-powerful. No healing is too hard for him, no demon dares to think of resistance.[24] Typically enough, the three Marcan narratives mentioned are missing in Matthew.[25]

The evangelist has, however, taken up the tradition of an exorcism in the region of the Decapolis. In Matthew (8: 28—34), the event takes place in the area of Gadara and concerns two demoniacs. They are fierce, and no-one dares pass their way. In Mark (5: 1—20) there is resistance and

---

[24] Theissen enumerates 17 items, which in Matthew stress the sovereignty of Jesus, *Wundergeschichten*, 178—180.

[25] Matthew seems to prefer omitting a narrative in the tradition to reworking it too radically, Held, *Matthäus*, 195—199.

a duel of words. Not so with Matthew, where no real dialogue arises. The demons immediately sense that they are outmatched and, faced with the mighty *exousia* of Jesus, they immediately prepare for *flight*. All they beg is to be given a refuge somewhere else — in a herd of swine. Jesus' word (ὑπάγετε, "Begone!") is not a command but a concession.[26] The spirits have their demonic wish fulfilled and at once rush to their destruction (cf. 6.5. below). This is the closest approach Matthew can make to a popular style when telling of Jesus.

Matthew's interest in possession by demons and in exorcism is, in fact, rather limited. The story of the Gadarene swine is the only traditional narrative of a detailed, concretely exorcistic type that he takes up. He mentions four further individual cases of exorcism, but in these pericopes only the fact is established: that the demon is cast out (9: 32—34), that he is rebuked and comes out (17: 14—18), and that the sick person is healed (12: 22—32, 15: 21—28). For Matthew, it is not natural to any great extent to see diseases as caused by demons and to regard Jesus as an exorcist.[27]

3.7. *Further aspects of the question of faith*

The picture Matthew paints of the therapeutic Jesus is very clear in one respect: his ministry is public and directed outward. Neither in the summaries nor in the narratives of the concrete miracles is anything said about any of the *disciples* being healed.[28] The therapeutic activity is one part — and an essential part — of the ministry of Jesus to Israel and to individual Israelites (after the Passover extended to the Gentiles). By Israel is meant in this case that part of Israel that is open to Jesus, not the inflexible leaders and those who follow them.

An important aspect of the therapeutic miracles is that they are worked on demand.[29] There seem to be only three exceptions. It seems as if Jesus heals spontaneously, on his own initiative, in two cases, that of Peter's mother-in-law and that of the man with the withered hand; at all events it is not said in these brief stories that he is asked. And in the case of the Gadarene demoniacs it is a question of a clash between Jesus and the two

---

[26] "All element of struggle, of menace, of tension is gone. The spirits have not been exorcized by a wonder worker; they have perished for ever before the face of Messiah", Hull, *Hellenistic Magic*, 132. Cf. Held, *Matthäus*, 162—165.

[27] See, besides the literature in notes 2: 11 and 6: 14, Hull, *Hellenistic Magic*, 128—141.

[28] Part of the explanation — although hardly all of it — is certainly to be found in the ideas about the divine "blessing"; if God "is with" a man, he is protected against all sorts of danger: he "shall not want", "nothing shall hurt" him. Cf. e.g. the formulations in Mk 16: 17—18, Lk 10: 17—19, Acts 28: 3—5. Therefore the disciples are always treated as healthy. On the "blessing" motif, see my studies *The Testing of God's Son (Matt 4: 1—11 & Par)*, part I, Lund 1966, *Jésus livré* (Intr.: 7) and *Gottes Sohn* (ibid.).

[29] Cf. Fridrichsen, *Le problème* (2: 13), 52, Eng. transl. 78—79.

demoniacs, at which the demons flee in face of the superior adversary. Here, Jesus is never asked to intervene.[30] In the other eleven cases, however, Jesus' intervention is *asked for*, usually in explicit words but sometimes only by actions. In these cases the evangelist is concerned to show that the supplicant turns to Jesus in faith (πιστεύειν, πίστις). The pattern is not that the miracle happens and awakens faith but that faith demands and is given the miracle.

The faith of the supplicants is expressed very clearly in the explicit words they utter in the concrete healing narratives; we have accounted for these utterances above. Matthew, however, also perceives the simple, silent appeal to Jesus as a supplicatory faith (*Gebetsglaube*) whose request is granted. It is expressly said in the narrative of the paralytic: "when Jesus saw their faith . . ." (9:1—8). And the same assessment of the appeals to Jesus is obviously implied in those cases where it is said that one or many sick persons are *brought to* Jesus (whether in the summaries or in concrete narratives). Of course it is quite natural to interpret the fact that someone brings along a sick person to Jesus as a plea for help. It could, however, just as well be a question of desperation as of faith. But Matthew always has Jesus interpret these appeals positively, as the plea of faith for help, a plea which directly and with no delay receives its benevolent answer.[31]

In two cases — when it is a question of Gentiles, who according to the historical rules of salvation do not yet have access to the blessings which Jesus gives — Jesus makes difficulties: he tests the faith of the supplicants (8:5—13, 15:21—28). This does not happen, however, in any of the other statements or accounts of Jesus' healings. And even in these two cases, Jesus does not upbraid the supplicants — on the contrary, he praises their faith.

This fact is striking: Matthew finds exemplary faith in the supplicants, and none of them are disciples — at any rate, not yet.

The faith portrayed in these therapeutic narratives is of a certain type: it is the faith which is granted help in need, the faith that receives miracles. A comparison of the relevant places in Matthew shows a fairly clear picture of this faith. It is a simple confidence in the power of Jesus and in his will to help. It is also a faith that knows what it wants and which actively — in word or deed — expresses itself in making a plea to Jesus, often breaking down obstacles standing in its way. The traits of volition and activity are clearly emphasized. It is a question of a confidence in Jesus that expresses both a will and a fighting spirit.[32]

The pattern in these narratives is that it is done for man according to

---

[30] Cf. 4:27 below.
[31] Held, *Matthäus*, 264—276. Held uses the expression "Gebetsglaube".
[32] Held, *ibidem*.

his belief. Or, to put it in precise terms: Jesus allows the person who in faith begs his help to be given what he asks.[33]

This seems at the same time to be an important part of Matthew's general teaching on the subject of *prayer*. Much suggests that these pericopes, which explicitly treat of the meeting of supplicants and Jesus, are the concrete material with which Matthew illustrates such maxims of Jesus as "Ask, and it will be given you . . ." (7: 7—11), and "And whatever you ask in prayer, you will receive, if you have faith . . ." (21: 22).[34]

To conclude with, I just want to mention quite briefly two important complexes of problems for further investigation. (1) We have seen how closely healing and teaching are related in Matthew. This gives us reason to ask: To what extent is Jesus conceived of as the healer of Israel even *in the teaching material* in Matthew? It is said expressly in one place (13: 15) that the acceptance of the teaching of Jesus is *healing*. (2) It seems more than likely that the material concerning the healing activity of Jesus has deeper dimensions. Jesus not only cures bodies, he makes men "whole". Certainly Matthew sees these pictures of healing as pictures of *"salvation"* in a fuller sense as well. The healer of Israel is the saviour of Israel. These two questions open wide perspectives, which we must, however, leave untouched.

---

[33] The common opinion (Bultmann, *Geschichte*, 234), that in the miracle narratives "belief" simply means confidence in the miracle-worker, is far from adequate regarding Matthew. Cf. Held, *ibidem*, and Theissen, *Wundergeschichten*, 62—64, 84, 133—143, 279, 291—293.

[34] Held, *Matthäus*, 268—272.

4. The pericopes of Jesus' non-therapeutic miracles

The synoptic tradition not only tells of Jesus healing the sick and driving out demons. It also contains accounts of other mighty acts, which Jesus is claimed to have done during his ministry in Israel. Following on from Bultmann, it has long been usual to call these remarkable works "nature miracles" (*Naturwunder*). Many scholars, however, have rightly criticised this designation, which seems rather to be based on the assessment of the modern historian of what is possible and what is not possible than on the formal structures and view of the world evident in the material itself.[1] I shall content myself, in what follows, with the general designation "non-therapeutic miracles."

4.1. *The material*

In the Gospel of Matthew, the following are the pericopes concerned:
1. Jesus calms the storm, 8: 23—27 (Mark 4: 35—41, Luke 8: 22—25)
2. Jesus feeds 5 000 men, 14: 13—21 (Mark 6: 30—44, Luke 9: 10—17)
3. Jesus walks on the sea, 14: 22—33 (Mark 6: 45—52), which includes the not entirely independent pericope 4:
4. Jesus enables Peter to walk on the water, 14: 28—31
5. Jesus feeds 4 000 men, 15: 29—39 (Mark 8: 1—10)
6. Jesus curses a fig tree, 21: 18—22 (Mark 11: 12—14, 20—25).

For practical reasons I add one borderline case to this list:
7. Jesus promises a coin in the mouth of a fish, 17: (24—)25b—27; in this text the miracle is not told but only foretold.

Five of the seven pericopes belong to what we call the Marcan material, and none to the Q material. Numbers 4 and 7 are only in Matthew. In Luke — remarkably enough — there are only nos. 1 and 2. The seven pericopes are in Matthew chapters 8—21; three of them are in a series in 14: 13—33.

---

[1] For the discussion about this, see R. Bultmann, *Die Geschichte der synoptischen Tradition. Ergänzungsheft*[4] (rev. by G. Theissen & P. Vielhauer), Göttingen 1971, 84. Cf. also Theissen, *Wundergeschichten* (Intr.: 2), 122—123, and Moule, *Miracles* (Intr.: 2), 239—243.

4.2. *The form*

The formal traits we noted in the pericopes of the therapeutic miracles (3.3. above) are also found in this material. The central secrets which Matthew wants to bring out are usually expressed in the *dialogue* found in each pericope.

As usual, the tightness of the structure is striking. B. Frid has shown [2] what a consistent *inclusio* structure has been given to the story of the calming of the storm in Matthew (8: 23—27):

- And when he got into the boat, his disciples followed him.
- And behold, there arose a great storm on the sea,
- so that the boat was being swamped by the waves;
- but he was asleep.
- And they went and woke him, saying: 'Save, Lord; we are perishing.'
- And he said to them: 'Why are you afraid, O men of little faith?'
- Then he rose
- and rebuked the winds and the sea;
- and there was a great calm.
- And the men marvelled, saying: 'Of what sort is this [man], that even winds and sea obey him?'

Here too, a comparison with the parallel versions (Mark 4: 35—41, Luke 8: 22—25) shows that the story certainly can be given a different form, and that the Matthean form is the result of highly conscious structural work. And here too one can make surprising discoveries concerning minute details of the shaping. The middle point of the pericope lies between the disciples' prayer and Jesus' reply. Before this point there are 83 syllables, and after it there are also 83.[3] I only give this example. (Cf. 3.3. above.)

4.3. *The persons*

The gallery of figures in these pericopes is simple. That which happens is played out between *Jesus* and *the disciples* (sometimes only one of them, Peter). There are no roles besides these two (J and Di) in the stories of the calming of the storm, the walking on the sea, Peter walking on the water, the cursing of the fig tree and the promise of the coin in the mouth of the fish.[4] Only in the two pericopes of the feeding miracles are the crowds (C) also included — but typically enough they are only in the

---

[2] The study has not yet been published. — X. Léon-Dufour, La tempête apaisée, *Nouv. Rev. Théol.* 97 (1965), 910—911, proposes another structure.

[3] I read πλοῖον without the article in v. 23.

[4] The tax-collectors in the beginning of the last mentioned pericope (17: 24—27) do not belong to the dialogue about the miracle (vv. 25 b—27), only to the prelude to this (vv. 24—25 a).

background, unaware of the miracle. The adversaries (A) are not given any connection with any of these miracles. Jesus is always mentioned first except in the prelude to the statement about the coin.

What we have established here seems to be of great importance for the interpretation of these pericopes. As opposed to the therapeutic miracles which are worked throughout for the people outside the group of the disciples — the crowds and individuals — while the disciples are not even mentioned (except in three cases), the non-therapeutic miracles are always worked for *the disciples* (or for one of them). They happen, so to speak, within the church. It seems to me that Matthew has seen these miraculous events as revelations, clarifying mysteries of the Reign for the disciples. They are, if I my put it thus, internal church miracles.

4.4. *The individual pericopes*

There are greater dissimilarities between the different pericopes of the non-therapeutic miracles than between the comparatively uniform healing stories. To avoid imposing too much uniformity on them when I am now about to bring out the central themes common to them, I shall first comment briefly on each in turn.

Held has been successful in indicating three main themes in these miracle stories: Christology, faith and discipleship.[5] It seems that much can be placed under these three headings, and I shall consider them to some extent in what follows. Personally, however, I prefer to give a more varied account of Matthew's view of *Jesus Christ and the relationship to him*, and especially the relationship between him and the disciples' faith, and between his *exousia* and that of the disciples.

4.4.1. *The calming of the storm,*
8: 23—27 (Mk 4: 35—41, Lk 8: 22—25)

What in Mark is a vivid story is in Matthew an instructional text with a tight structure (cf. 4.2. above). The main points of the pericope are revealed both in the two utterances in the middle of it — the disciples' plea for help and Jesus' reply — and in the almost confessional utterance at the end. The miracle described is of the "epiphany and saving" type.[6] Jesus reveals a glimpse of his divine power and glory at the same time as saving the disciples from shipwreck.

The marked *Christological* interest of the narrator is obvious. The pericope ends with "the men" — probably the disciples [7] — reacting with

---

[5] Held, *Matthäus* (Intr.: 4), Cf. e.g. S. Legasse, Les miracle de Jésus selon Matthieu, in Léon-Dufour, *Miracles* (Intr.: 2), 227—247, Fuller, *Interpreting* (3: 4), 77—82.

[6] Cf. Theissen, *Wundergeschichten*, 102—111. Theissen's designation is "rettende Epiphanie", 109.

[7] "The men" in v. 27 are according to Léon-Dufour (*Tempête*, 90—91) the outsiders,

wonder and saying, "Of what sort (ποταπός) is this [man], that even winds and sea obey him?" The power of Jesus over the elements thus shows what an extraordinary *exousia* he has and suggests the direction in which the secret of his person should be sought.

Corresponding to the Christological theme is the theme of *faith*. If Jesus possesses this supreme power over the elements, his followers need have no fear of wind and wave. In the story, however, the disciples show no faith or trust in his company but act in such a way that Jesus has to rebuke them for being fearful and of little faith. The two utterances in the centre of the pericope are revealing here.

As Bornkamm and Held have shown, the intention of this pericope in the Gospel of Matthew is also to give more general instruction on the conditions of *discipleship*, on the situation of Jesus' followers (the church) in the world. This is not clearly expressed in the utterances in the pericope, but it is suggested in other ways. Matthew has preceded this story with two pronouncement stories concerning discipleship (8: 18—22). He has also formulated the introduction to the portrayal of the calming of the storm so that it now says that Jesus gets into the boat and the disciples follow (ἀκολουθεῖν) him. The situation of the boat and the disciples on the lake is also delineated so as to suggest symbolically the situation of the church in the world.[8] This theme — that of discipleship — is suggested, however, more through the general shaping of the story, through certain formulations and through its place in the context than through its explicit content. This theme is thus not a foreground theme in this Matthean pericope.

4.4.2. (a) *The feeding of 5 000 men*,
14: 13—21 (Mk 6: 32—44, Lk 9: 10—17)

(b) *The feeding of 4 000 men*,
15: 29—39 (Mk 8: 1—10)

The two stories of the feeding miracles are short and stringently built up in Matthew, and they are also more alike than are the two parallels in Mark. Both have a prelude showing how the crowds' hunger arises: they have been with Jesus for a long time in a lonely place (see 2.3.3. above).

In the first story (a) the disciples receive express instructions from Jesus to give the crowds something to eat. Jesus says to them, "They (the crowds) need not go away (to buy food for themselves); you give them something to eat." And Jesus also renders them capable of carrying out this order. The miracle itself is not portrayed, but its huge dimensions are

---

"the world"; according to Bornkamm (see next note) and Theissen (*Wundergeschichten*, 166—167), those who listen to this narrative in the preaching of the church.

[8] Thus G. Bornkamm in his famous essay Die Sturmstillung im Matthäusevangelium, in *Überlieferung* (Intr.: 4), 48—53. Cf. Held, *Matthäus*, 189—192, 253—254, Léon-Dufour, *Tempête*, and many others.

suggested by the information at the end that there were twelve full baskets left over after the meal, and that so many had eaten and been satisfied (5 000 men, besides women and children). There is nothing to suggest that the crowds are aware that anything miraculous is taking place. Neither is anything said of the disciples' reaction to the miracle, but their awareness of what has happened is probably implied.

The second story (b) has become very similar to the first — certainly under the hand of Matthew: see especially the preludes, and also the endings which are rendered in almost the same words. The mention of the fish has been reduced to a minimum in both stories (cf. Mark).[9] One difference between (a) and (b) is that in the former it is the disciples and in the latter it is Jesus himself who brings up the problem of the crowd's hunger.

The evangelist has constructed no bridge between the two feeding miracles (from the genetic point of view, what we have here must be two variants of the same tradition). A miraculous feeding is just as far from the disciples' thoughts in the second story as it is in the first. The evangelist does not let the disciples remember a single scrap from one occasion to the next.

The two stories have, on the other hand, been given something as rare as an explicit commentary in a quite different pericope in the gospel: 16: 5—12 (Mark 8: 14—21). It is typical that the disciples have forgotten here as well: they do not remember what they have experienced. Jesus has to remind them of how little trouble it was to solve the food question in the cases when the 5 000 and 4 000 were fed. This is done to obviate the disciples' want of understanding and their worry about food in the ordinary sense. This commentary shows that Matthew is taking our pericopes primarily as texts on bodily hunger and feeding, and not mainly in a symbolic sense.

The miracle is most nearly of the "gift miracle" (*Geschenkwunder*) type.[10] To be more precise, one can perhaps say that in this case the miracle is an example to show what *exousia* Jesus has and gives to the disciples. He does not only command, he also gives them power and ability to carry out the task he gives them, which by human standards is apparently impossible. Perhaps one can call what is told here an "*exousia* miracle". The *Christology* supports as usual what is presented here. It is striking, however, what a central role is assigned in these pericopes to the *followers*, the disciples. We shall return to this, and also to the theme of *faith* (4.5.—6.).

Commentators usually point out the unmistakable allusions to the Eucharist — and also to the manna theme and the great theme of the Bread of Life — which the pericope contains. This is obviously true. The

---

[9] See further Held, *Matthäus*, 171—177.
[10] On the "*Geschenkwunder*", see Theissen, *Wundergeschichten*, 111—114.

primary concern, however, as we have already pointed out, is the actual satisfying feeding of hungry people. In Matthew's time the Eucharist had probably not yet been made fully distinct from the satiating common meals in the early Christian communities. Thus eucharistic symbolism does not exclude the possibility that the story is concerned with the satisfaction of elementary bodily hunger — and *vice versa*.

4.4.3. (a) *The walking on the sea*,
14: 22—33 (Mk 6: 45—52), which includes

(b) *Peter's walking on the water*,
14: 28—31 (not in Mark)

Matthew has not needed to adapt the basic story (a) to any great extent. The introduction to the pericope states the necessary conditions for the event — how the distance arises between Jesus and the disciples. The disciples are in need in the dark on the stormy waves when Jesus comes to them "walking on the sea". When they misunderstand the situation he tells them, "Take heart, it is I; have no fear." This is the central pronouncement of the pericope and it stands, typically enough, in the exact centre of the double story. The miraculous elements are that Jesus comes to his disciples walking on the sea, and that he achieves the calming of the storm. The miracle is of the "epiphany and saving" type.

It is quite clear that the main point of the basic story is a *Christological* one. The significance and effect of the event is stated in the concluding words on the disciples' reaction: *proskynesis* and a confession of faith, "Truly you are the Son of God!" We can see how important this point is for the evangelist by the fact that here, unlike Mark, he breaks the general arrangement of his gospel. The confession of the disciples should not really come until the Caesarea-Philippi pericope (16: 13—20). — As for the theme of *faith*, we shall return to that later (4.6.).

What is portrayed in the basic story takes place in a framework as it were within the church — it is about Jesus and his closest followers. It is even clearer how this framework applies to the episode which Matthew has intercalated, namely (b) Peter's walking on the water. In the first half of this episode, Jesus makes Peter able to walk on the water, and he can. In the second half the disciple is unsuccessful and Jesus has to save him. Both halves, incidentally, are of exactly the same length, with 69 syllables each. The spoken words are also decisive in the intercalated episode.

The *Christology* provides the basis for what is told. Peter cannot walk on the water but Jesus — who can — gives him the command and the ability. The miracle is an "*exousia* miracle". The relationship between Jesus' "own" power and the disciples' "borrowed" power is very well expressed by Jesus' epiphanic words "It is I" (ἐγώ εἰμι) being taken up by

Peter's "Lord, if it is you . . ." And the difference between the divine Jesus — he who stands — and the mortal Peter — he who falls — is delineated with perfectly apparent symbolism in the second part of the episode. The theme of *faith* is something I shall take up in a short while (4.6.).

The concluding reaction — the disciples' *proskynesis* and confession of faith (v. 33) — primarily belongs to the basic story but is probably also an allusion back to the secondary side episode with Peter. Note how the two men on the water are brought together in the narrative in the formulation "when they got into the boat" (v. 32).

As in the pericope of the calming of the storm, the disciples' situation in this double story is delineated in such a way that it is certainly intended to symbolize the situation of the church in the world and so serve for instruction, admonition and comfort for the "followers" of Jesus.[11]

4.4.4. *The cursing of the fig tree*, 21:18—22 (Mk 11:12—14, 20—25)

In Mark, this story is split, with other material between the two parts. The fig tree does not wither away immediately — it is not until the following morning that the disciples notice that this has happened. In Matthew the pericope is shaped as a single unit. Jesus' words of power take immediate effect. The miraculous nature of the occurrence is clearly brought out: the disciples marvel (θαυμάζειν) and ask how Jesus' action could be possible (v. 20). This gives Jesus a reason to teach in plain words what endless resources of power the disciples have if they have faith.

This pericope is the only one in the gospels where Jesus' power is used in a destructive manner. It is misleading, however, to call the action a "punishment miracle" (*Strafwunder*).[12] Jesus is not punishing the tree. His action is meant as a visual illustration for his prophetic teaching.

In the original form of the story, Jesus' action was in all probability interpreted as a prophetic symbolic action, intended to show that the judgment will fall without mercy on a people or a city (Israel or Jerusalem) which bears no fruit to God at the time of visitation, the time of the Messiah.[13] I find it hard to believe that Matthew should have abandoned this interpretation of Jesus' action completely; it certainly still survived. In the present form of the pericope, however, a different interpretation

---

[11] For the most recent study of the narrative of Jesus walking on the sea (in Mark), see J. Delorme, L'intégration des petites unités littéraires dans l'Évangile de Marc du point de vue de la sémiotique structurale, *New Test. Stud.* 25 (1978—79), 469—491. — On the Old Testament-Jewish background of the story of Peter's walking on the water, see E. Lövestam, Wunder und Symbolhandlung. Eine Studie über Matthäus 14, 28—31, *Ker. und Dogma* 8 (1962), 124—135.

[12] Thus Theissen, *Wundergeschichten*, 117.

[13] Cf. G. Münderlein, Die Verfluchung des Feigenbaumes (Mk. XI. 12—14), *New Test. Stud.* 10 (1963—64), 88—104.

has, so to speak, been superimposed on the original one and thus been given priority. Jesus' cursing of the fig tree — one may even call it an *"exousia miracle"* — is a didactic demonstrative action intended to show that he who "has faith and has no doubts" can do such mighty acts, and even move mountains with his word alone. This means that the *Christological* (and eschatological) significance has been pushed into the background in favour of a more general ecclesiastical interpretation indicating the possibilities of the *followers* if they only have faith.

It is noteworthy that only the *disciples'* faith is being talked about, never Jesus' faith.[14] This corresponds to the conviction that he has his "own" *exousia*, while theirs is "borrowed" from him.

The fact that this bold instruction is linked to such a paltry example as the withering of a fig tree shows to what an extent the two evangelists are bound to tradition. Had they felt free to invent they would surely have had Jesus move the Mount of Olives or perform some action of similar dimensions.

4.4.5. *The coin in the fish's mouth*, 17: (24—)25b—27

This pericope — which is only in Matthew — is a borderline case. It is doubtful if it should be counted among the pericopes of the mighty acts of Jesus. For one thing, the miracle is not portrayed as something which occurs but is merely promised, and for another it is not said expressly that *Jesus* will work it; perhaps he is only anticipating a miraculous event with prophetic foresight. Jesus' words are also given in an imaginative, pictorial, haggadic style.[15] The evangelist does not mention any reaction to the words about the miracle. I am including this pericope, but only as a doubtful borderline case.

What is remarkable about the miracle that is promised here is that it is intended to benefit Jesus himself.[16] Otherwise, it is a consistent principle — from the temptation after the baptism to the death on the cross — that Jesus does not use his miraculous power for his own needs. The reason why this happens in this pericope is probably that Jesus is here brought together with Peter. The miracle that is promised is to benefit Peter, but only because he belongs together with Jesus. The *Christology* and the teaching concerning the situation of the *disciples* are held together and allowed to borrow elements from each other. The promised miracle is of the "gift miracle" type.[17]

The words about the miracle which are relevant for us are quite short and are found in the pronouncement of Jesus which concludes the story

---

[14] Cf. Held, *Matthäus*, 180, 277—278.
[15] Cf. Richardson, *Miracle-Stories* (3: 2), 105—108.
[16] M. Dibelius characterizes this miracle as "miraculous self-help" (*wunderbare Selbsthilfe*), and Bultmann agrees, *Geschichte* (3: 15), 233.
[17] Cf. note 10 above.

of the temple tax (v. 27). This pericope — from the form-critical point of view one of the type usually called pronouncement stories (*Apophthegmata*), or to be more precise a school dialogue (*Schulgespräch*) — treats of a concrete problem: the attitude which Jesus and his (Jewish) disciples are to take towards the temple tax. In the introduction to the pericope (vv. 17—25a), the question is whether Jesus himself pays this tax, but the perspective is then widened to include Peter as well, and indeed all who are counted as the "sons (of God)" (vv. 25b—26). Jesus teaches Peter and tells him very clearly that the sons of God are freed from the tax to God's temple — they are just as free as the sons of a king are from paying tax to their father the king. To avoid giving offence, however, they should pay tax in any case. The promise of a coin in the mouth of a fish (v. 27) seems to be intended to show that the sons of God — Jesus and Peter (and others in their situation), who work in the service of God without salary on earth — will be provided with money for the temple tax through God's special providence. The last mentioned element of the pericope invites a symbolic interpretation: the fishers of men (4: 19) are to receive money for the temple tax from those whom they win for the gospel (cf. the Gentile Christians' collection for "the holy ones" in Jerusalem).

What we meet with here is an internal church problem, solved within a Christian frame of reference: is one as a (Jewish) Christian to pay the temple tax or not? The words about the miracle seem to answer an uneasy objection: how will it be possible for those who "have left everything"?

4.5. *The main theme of the pericopes:*
the exousia *of Jesus and the disciples*

The *therapeutic* miracles are fairly uniform and regular. The supplicants beg Jesus for something (healing), they believe that he can grant their request and he does so. The miracles are expected, and they are worked on demand. Here, Jesus' *exousia* is portrayed, but in its public, well-known aspect — his power of healing.

As far as the non-therapeutic miracles are concerned, the situation is different. Here, Jesus reveals his *exousia* to his disciples on his own initiative, and in an unexpected and surprising manner. Here, the miracles are of different types (two are miracles of epiphany and saving, two are *exousia* miracles, and three are gift miracles): through various events, hitherto unknown sides of Jesus' *exousia* are revealed.

In the two feeding stories, it is quite beyond the horizon of the disciples to imagine that Jesus and they should be able to feed the great throngs out in the wilderness with the very small supply of food they have. The miracle comes entirely unexpectedly; likewise in the second feeding story. In the pericope of walking on the water, the disciples have no idea that it is Jesus coming to them "walking on the sea". When the fig tree withers under the words of Jesus, the disciples marvel and ask how this could happen. In the story of the calming of the storm the miracle is, it is true, worked on demand, but the prayer of the disciples is so to speak an open one and help comes in a marvellous form which causes them to wonder what sort of man this is, that even winds and sea obey him. The coin in the mouth of the fish is promised quite unexpectedly. Only in the story of how Peter walks on the water is the miracle worked directly on specific request, but this does not happen before Jesus — on his own initiative and in an entirely unexpected manner — has revealed that he has power over wind and waves. This is how new sides of Jesus' *exousia* are revealed: it is greater and richer than his disciples have understood and believed.

A further important aspect of these pericopes is that the disciples are presumed to share in the divine "blessing" and extraordinary *exousia* of Jesus. This is not merely revealed to them.[18]

In the feeding stories, the main emphasis is in fact on the *disciples'* task of feeding crowds.[19] In the first of these, Jesus expressly gives the disciples the task of giving food to the crowds. In the second, they take the feeding as their business: "Where are we (*sic*) to get bread enough in the desert to feed so great a crowd?" And Jesus enables them to carry out the miraculous feeding. In both stories, Matthew then uses the formulation that Jesus "gave (the food) to the disciples, and the disciples gave (it) to the crowds". In the pericope of how Jesus walks on the sea, the episode of Peter has been intercalated in Matthew: the disciple is given Jesus' command to exercise the same miraculous power as that which Jesus exercises. In the story of the fig tree, Jesus performs the miracle but following on from that he teaches the disciples that they can do the same things, and indeed work even greater miracles than this. For them, however, one precondition is stated — that they have faith and have no doubts. This need not be stated for his part; he is, so to speak, one with his *exousia*, whereas their *exousia* can be said to be "borrowed". The coin in the mouth of the fish is promised as an extraordinary benefit not only for Jesus but also for Peter; the one who gives Peter the directive also has marvellous resources to offer. It is only in the pericope of the calming of the storm that this does not appear quite clearly. We can hardly be mistaken, however, if we consider it to be implied. When Jesus rebukes the disciples for being afraid in his boat, this may reasonably be taken to presuppose that his power over wind and waves protects them as well; they share Jesus'

---

[18] Cf. Held, *Matthäus*, 276—278, who characterizes faith as "Anteilhaben an Jesu Wundermacht", and A. Suhl, *Die Wunder Jesu. Ereignis und Überlieferung*, Gütersloh 1968, 36—37, who uses the expression "Anteil an der Allmacht Gottes".

[19] Held, *Matthäus*, 171—177.

immunity to all kinds of danger.[20] This implies presumably also that they have access to his *exousia*.[21]

4.6. Faith

As we have seen, the non-therapeutic miracle stories are about Jesus and the *disciples*. One of the striking aspects is that the disciples' attitude in all these stories — disregarding the item about the coin in the fish's mouth — is presented as *problematic*. Jesus has to open their eyes and in several cases take them to task. They do not show the insight and faith which Jesus expects of them, but time and again reveal their want of faith.

The rare adjective ὀλιγόπιστος ("of little faith") and the substantive ὀλιγοπιστία (*hapax*, "little faith") are only used of the disciples (6: 30, 8: 26, 14: 31, 16: 8 and 17: 20). This designates a faith that is little, frail and unsteady. It also incorporates, or is intimately connected with, the inability to *understand* the boundlessness of Jesus' *exousia* and thus also what a boundless *exousia* the disciples themselves have access to. The contrasting ideal seems to be the "great" faith (15: 28), that is to say an unlimited, solid faith in Jesus and his cause.[22]

We shall now consider the pericopes in turn. It is part of the pattern that in each case the problem-situation is caused by Jesus. As we have already pointed out, the non-therapeutic miracle stories are all concerned with the situation among Jesus' followers, that is to say with problems of the disciples.

1. *The calming of the storm*. In Matthew the boat passage is Jesus' voyage, the disciples following him. The stormy sea brings desperation to the disciples and they are obliged to beg help of Jesus. He rebukes them for being afraid, calls them "men of little faith" — and saves them. The implication must be that they are in safety when they are together with him whom both winds and sea obey, but that they have neither understood this nor believed it.

2. *The feeding of the 5 000*. The emergency situation for the crowds has been caused by Jesus. The people have come to him and stayed with him all day. It is not the disciples but the crowds who are in an emergency situation, but it becomes a *problem* for the disciples. They are given the command by Jesus to feed the hungry crowds. They do not take this to mean that miraculous resources will be at their disposal. Without the actual word being given in the text, the narrator here gives a picture of incomprehension in face of the task "Give them something to eat". This incomprehension certainly also implies that they are men "of little faith".

---

[20] See note 3: 28 above.
[21] Cf. Theissen, *Wundergeschichten*, 107—111.
[22] Cf. e.g. G. Barth, Das Gesetzesverständnis des Evangelisten Matthäus, in *Überlieferung* (Intr.: 4), 105—108, 110—113, and Held, *Matthäus*, 194—195, 278—284.

3. *The walking on the water*. The voyage is undertaken on the initiative of Jesus: he compels the disciples to put out on to the lake, where the boat is seriously threatened by the waves. When he then comes to them, they cry out in terror without understanding that it is the powerful and help-giving Jesus who is coming to them. Their fear — which discloses incomprehension — should certainly be interpreted, as in verses 30—31, as showing that they are "men of little faith".

4. *Peter walking on the water*. Jesus commands Peter to walk on the water as he is doing himself. Peter makes a successful beginning: both his plea and his walking on the water show that he has faith. But "when he sees the wind" he is seized by fear and begins to sink. Jesus rebukes him for his doubt (διστάζειν) and calls him a "man of little faith".

5. *The feeding of the 4 000*. Here, too, the hunger-situation is caused by Jesus; this time the crowd has stayed with him for three days. It is the people and not the disciples who are hungry, but the disciples have the task of solving the problem, of relieving the need. The role of the disciples is not so clearly delineated here, however, as in the first feeding story. But in this portrayal as well, the miracle is beyond the horizon of the disciples' thoughts. The evangelist does not allow them to remember anything at all of the previous feeding miracle. So they reveal their incomprehension — and presumably also that they are "men of little faith".

6. *The cursing of the fig tree*. Jesus is hungry, but this is not an emergency situation for him — the story does not continue by describing how Jesus' hunger was satisfied; it is simply the point of departure for his subsequent action. That which causes the disciples to marvel and is therefore brought up as a problem is the question of how something such as the immediate withering of the fig tree was possible. Jesus answers with a lesson on what the disciples can achieve — typically enough, through *their word* — if they "have faith and have no doubts (μὴ διακριθῆτε)", and on what the boundless power of prayer can achieve if the prayer is made in faith.

7. *The coin in the fish's mouth*. Here, though there is no situation of need, there is surely a problem for Jesus and his disciples. In the brief pronouncement about the coin we do not find the theme of incomprehension and want of faith. It is not inconceivable, however, that the promise of the coin corresponds to an imagined question, where an uneasy and doubting Peter wonders where they are to find the money for the temple tax which is to be paid.

In the stories of the therapeutic miracles, as we have seen in the previous chapter, the evangelist emphasizes the faith of the *supplicants*. This is presented throughout as *unproblematic*. Jesus never has to rebuke them for want of understanding or of faith. They are exemplary. In this chapter we have now seen how the faith of the *disciples* is treated in the stories of the non-therapeutic miracles. It is presented throughout as *problematic*. They appear as feeble in the matter of understanding and feeble in the matter of faith. They are warning examples rather than examples to be followed. Perhaps the perspective is that they are *not yet* equal to their task.

It is important to note, however, that the two different groups of stories are concerned with two different types of faith,[23] or rather, of *different aspects of faith*. In the pericopes of the therapeutic miracles it is a question of elementary, fundamental faith: the faith which demands help and is allowed to receive help in its need. In the pericopes of the non-therapeutic miracles, on the other hand, it is as a rule a question of the faith which is to work miracles itself. The faith of the miracle-worker, so to speak. Or, to be more precise, the faith which the disciples of Jesus need to enable them to carry out the miraculous tasks Jesus has given them — to enable the *exousia* which they have received from Jesus to function. Perhaps we could call it the faith in their ministry.

Thus it is a question of two different aspects of faith in Jesus Christ — the faith of the miracle-receiver and that of the miracle-worker. The connection between the two is not hard to see. Faith is required both in the supplicants who come to the disciples (the church) and in those who on behalf of Jesus are to help these people in a need which can only be relieved by mighty acts.

One pericope is especially illuminating in this connection, because it so clearly makes a bridge between these two aspects of belief in Christ. This is a pericope which, although it treats of a *therapeutic* miracle, still — and this is a rather original situation — places the problems of the *disciples* in the foreground: the pericope of the healing of the epileptic boy (17: 14—20). Here, a man in need of help has turned to Jesus' disciples on behalf of his sick son, but the disciples have not been able to cure him. Jesus heaves a heavy sigh over them — "O faithless and perverse generation, how long am I to be with you?" — and then explains privately to the disciples that their failure is because of their "little faith" (ὀλιγοπιστία). Typically enough, the blame is not laid on the supplicant. His faith is not disputed. The blame is laid on the disciples; their faith is not what it should be, a constantly effective, miracle-working faith. Here we see both the difference and the connection between the two aspects of faith.

It is a bitter explanation that the Matthean Jesus gives of the fact that the church can not perform all the miracles which she should be able to work in the name of Jesus. Matthew does not allow Jesus to refer to inscrutable secrets: the mystery of evil, God's unfathomable plans or

---

[23] Cf. Held, who makes the distinction between "der Glaube als Gebetsglaube" and "der Glaube als Anteilhaben an Jesu Wundermacht", *Matthäus*, 272—278.

something else that is impenetrable to human thought.[24] The blame is laid on the church: it is weak in its faith.[25]

One point should perhaps be added. There are naturally points of contact between the need of the supplicants in the therapeutic stories and the problems of the disciples in the pericopes we are analysing here. In the stories of the calming of the storm and the walking on the sea the disciples are in elementary need and require elementary help. Otherwise, however, the differences are fairly clear. The supplicants in the therapeutic stories do not demand help to walk on the sea, to curse fig trees and move mountains or feed immense crowds with a few loaves and small fish. They demand help in their own broadly human need: their own sickness or that of someone close to them.

4.7. *Comparison with the therapeutic miracles*

To make the general outlines even clearer, I shall finally make a brief comparison with the pericopes of the therapeutic miracles (and, where appropriate, also with the summaries). This will be a collation of observations which, as a rule, have been made above, though widely spread out.

The stories of the non-therapeutic miracles seem to have been completely absent in the so-called Q material, in which at least one concrete therapeutic miracle is found (the centurion's servant).[26]

Considering the special character of the non-therapeutic miracles, it is not surprising that they are spread out through the gospel. Only one of them — which concerns help in elementary need (the calming of the storm) — has been given a place in the large miracle collection in chapters 8—9, where no less than nine of the fourteen therapeutic miracles are related.

The therapeutic miracles are portrayed as continually recurring, typical actions on the part of Jesus, as a main part of his ministry in Israel. The non-therapeutic miracles are occasional events, each a different and unique event apart from the *two* feeding miracles that are told.

The therapeutic miracles are, with only three possible exceptions, per-

---

[24] Cf. the conviction, expressed e.g. by Paul, that a prayer for healing may receive the answer "No" for some inscrutable higher reason: "My grace is sufficient for you, for my power is made perfect in weakness" (2 Cor 12: 7—10). — For this theme — the paradoxical weakness and failure of a man of God — see my studies *The Testing* (3: 28), passim, and the articles mentioned in Intr., note 7 above. Cf. also J. Jervell, Der schwache Charismatiker, in *Rechtfertigung* (*Festschrift* in honour of E. Käsemann), Tübingen & Göttingen 1976, 185—198.

[25] Matthew is, however, aware of the possibility that the fault may be with the people. He reports a case when even Jesus himself had to meet with this hindrance, 13: 54—58 (5.2.1. below).

[26] In the Q material we find not only a concrete miracle narrative (the centurion's servant) but also other material about Jesus' therapeutic miracles; see 5: 6 below.

formed on demand.[27] The non-therapeutic ones are worked on Jesus' own initiative, except in two cases (the calming of the storm and Peter's walking on the water).

It is striking that, in the short summaries as in the concrete pericopes, the therapeutic miracles are always performed for the people or for individual "outsiders", while the non-therapeutic miracles are always worked for the disciples or for one of them (Peter).

The difference is also apparent in the fact that the non-therapeutic miracles are not included in the summaries concerning Jesus' ministry, but only the therapeutic ones: also, in Matthew's items concerning the crowds' reactions to Jesus' mighty acts there are no allusions to the non-therapeutic miracles.

The same is true, incidentally, of the statements concerning the reactions of the adversaries; in no case do the controversies concern what is portrayed in the non-therapeutic miracle stories.

These facts are so apparent that one simple conclusion must be drawn from them: part of the generally known, *public* picture of Jesus was that he cured the sick and cast out evil spirits. Clearly, however, it was not according to Matthew a part of that picture that he did other kinds of marvellous acts. Everything suggests that the pericopes of the non-therapeutic miracles belong together with the faith experiences within the church and the internal Christian discussions of Jesus' *exousia* — and that of the church.

I shall not here discuss the questions of *historicity*. Such a discussion would naturally have to include the material of the other evangelists. I shall, however, note a few general reflections, as an appendix to what has already been said.

In the non-therapeutic stories it is harder to divine the historical basis than in the therapeutic ones. It is harder to know where the literal ends and the symbolic begins. One has a feeling of standing in the proximity of the *haggada* and the *mashal*.[28] The miraculous ability to move mountains and cause fig trees to wither on the spot must be conceived symbolically. This kind of action, taken literally, was not part of Jesus' mission. The fearless defiance of wind and waves, on the other hand, probably has a primarily literal significance. The person living in the modern technological, urban society can hardly have any feeling for the elemental threat posed by the violent forces of nature to people in former times. There was

---

[27] Cf. 3.7. above. The three possible exceptions are no strong evidence against the rule: The pericope concerning Peter's mother-in-law is extremely brief and concentrated upon a specific point; it might well be silently implied that Peter had asked Jesus to heal his relative. Considerations of a similar kind may be made on the story about the man with the withered hand. And as to the exorcism at Gadara: the demons can not reasonably be supposed to ask to be expelled.

[28] Cf. Richardson, *Miracle-Stories*, 105—108.

much comfort in the proclamation that Jesus was also lord of storm and sea. A symbolic significance probably also plays a part here, however. It was easy to glide over from these literal threats to the satanic and demonic forces behind them (the assaults of the devil and the evil spirits against Jesus' mission and Jesus' followers, "the powers of death" etc., and the attacks of human assailants against the church, "afflictions and persecutions",[29] etc.) and to think of Jesus' divine supremacy over such enemies. The power enabling him to feed hungry crowds is certainly also primarily literally conceived: bodily hunger was a hard reality in the historical milieu of Jesus and early Christianity. However, starting from the thought of the sacred communal meals and the Eucharist, here too the way was short to the great symbolical perspectives (the Bread of Life, etc.). The need of money for the temple tax must have been an actual problem for disciples without means but, as we have seen, a symbolic meaning is also easily found in Jesus' words on the coin in the fish's mouth.

It is hard to tell what feeling Matthew has for what may literally have happened and what is interpretation, praise, confession and proclamation. His picture of the unbounded power of Jesus has hardly made him "realistic" in our sense of the word. One thing is clear, however: when he writes he is more concerned to interpret, glorify, and proclaim the divine, saving power of Jesus than to be over-scrupulous in describing what originally happened. His "historiography" is *Christological*.

---

[29] Cf. Lövestam, *Wunder*, who points out that storms and waves in Jewish interpretation are often taken as symbols of hostile attacks on the people of God.

5. Material concerning resistance and controversies

In the three immediately preceding chapters we have examined the material which shows how Matthew represents the mighty acts of Jesus as he sees them himself. We shall now examine how he portrays the *resistance* to the thaumaturgical Jesus, and *the adversaries' negative interpretations* of his mighty acts. We shall firstly consider some texts which we have not examined before, and secondly we shall closely scrutinize a specific element in four of the texts on which we have already commented — the element concerning the adversaries' reactions to Jesus' mighty acts and, in three cases, the answers of Jesus (and the church) to these attacks. As has already been pointed out, this element is found only in four of the miracle stories. These are in each case healing narratives.

The examination prepares the question we pose in the concluding section (5.4.): To what extent may Matthew's presentation of the thaumaturgical ministry of Jesus be affected by apologetic considerations caused by the polemic of the adversaries?

5.1. *The material*

The following are the two groups of material we shall examine here:[1]

A. *Unreceptiveness and rejection*
1. The rejection in Nazareth, 13:54—58 (Mk 6:1—6, cf. Lk 4:16—30).
2. The impenitence in Chorazin, Bethsaida and Capernaum, 11:20—24 (Lk 10:13—15).

B. *Polemics of the adversaries*
1. Against the casting out of demons, 9:32—34, 12:22—31 (Mk 3:22—30, Lk 11:14—23, 12:10).
2. Against the forgiveness of sins, 9:1—8 (Mk 2:1—12, Lk 5:17—26).
3. Against healing on the sabbath, 12:9—14 (Mk 3:1—6, Lk 6:6—11).

5.2. *Unreceptiveness and rejection*

The total picture in the Gospel of Matthew as finally edited presupposes the conception that official Israel has definitively rejected Jesus. We need

---

[1] I do not discuss here the pericope about the exorcism at the Hellenistic Gadara (8:28—34), which ends with the statement that "all the city" begged Jesus to leave their neighbourhood. See Theissen, *Wundergeschichten* (Intr.: 2), 81, 149, 177, 252—253.

not examine this more closely: many scholars have written about it. Perhaps we should, however, actualize one important line in the evangelist's presentation: "the crowds" (οἱ ὄχλοι) assume an open, positive attitude to Jesus for a very long time. The swing in the other direction does not come until the scene in Gethsemane, where the crowds have made common cause with their leaders (26:47—56). Here it is surely a question of Jerusalem crowds, not the Galilean pilgrims who glorified him with hosannas at his entry into Jerusalem (21:1—11).[2] The swing becomes final at the trial before Pilate, when "the blind leaders" — that is how the evangelist sees them[3] — succeed in persuading the crowds (οἱ ὄχλοι) to choose Barabbas and reject Jesus (27:11—26). Here, finally, comes the accentuated expression "all the people" (πᾶς ὁ λαός, v. 25).

The picture of favourably disposed crowds is built up in different ways. For our purpose it is of particular interest to notice what an important role is played in this connection by the summaries (see chap. 2 above) — and also by many concrete pericopes on individual mighty acts (chap. 3, and also the sections on the feeding miracles in chap. 4).

There are, however, sections of text which even during the portrayal of Jesus' public ministry in Galilee draw a picture of unreceptive and rejective crowds: in the parable chapter (13:1—52), a dark contrast is painted between the receptive disciples and the unreceptive crowds, who do not turn to Jesus to be healed by him (v. 15). In this section in the middle of the Gospel we are thus given an independent overall vision; this corresponds to the overall vision at the end of the Gospel, not that of the presentation of the situation before Gethsemane. A similar picture of general, if not quite unanimous unreceptiveness is given in the concrete pericopes of Jesus' visit to his home town of Nazareth (13:54—58) and of his words of judgment over the three Galilean cities where he had done most of his mighty acts (11:20—24). We shall make a certain amount of comment on these from our point of view.

5.2.1. *The unreceptiveness in Nazareth*, 13:54—58 (Mk 6:1—6, Lk 4:16—30)

In the pericope on the failure of Jesus in Nazareth there is a pronouncement of Jesus at the centre: "A prophet is not without honour except in his own country and in his own house" (v. 57). The pericope is skilfully formed to illustrate this. Jesus comes to his original home town. There, the inhabitants do not give him a positive welcome but "take offence" (σκανδαλίζεσθαι) at him. Their negative reaction, which is expressed in direct

---

[2] "The crowds that went before him and that followed him shouted, 'Hosanna . . .'" (v. 9). This must refer to pilgrims, not to the inhabitants of Jerusalem ("all the city", v.10). — As to "the crowds" in Matthew, see 2:5 above.
[3] 15:14, 23:16, 17, 19, 24, 26. Cf. van Tilborg, *The Jewish Leaders* (2:5).

speech, applies to both the main aspects of his ministry, the teaching and the healing: "Where did this man get this wisdom (σοφία) and these mighty acts (δυνάμεις)?" (v. 54, cf. 56). The reason for the question is the very fact that he is a son of the town: the son of a woman in the town, and the brother of some men and women in the town. Jesus answers with the aphoristic pronouncement we have just quoted. And at the conclusion of the pericope it is summarily noted that he did not do many mighty acts there. The reason for this is expressly stated: "because of their unbelief (διὰ τὴν ἀπιστίαν αὐτῶν)" (v. 58).

The pronouncement of Jesus that has been preserved, suggests — with its application to Jesus himself — that his ministry was not successful in Nazareth. Historically speaking, this is certainly correct, whether we have to base our conclusions only on the actual pronouncement of Jesus (that is to say, if the pericope is just presenting "an ideal scene")[4] or can assume that a definite historical event lies behind the tautly structured narrative.

It is important to note that it is not said here that "the crowds" reject Jesus. What is portrayed is *the total reaction of his home town*. Those who express this rejective attitude towards the wisdom and mighty acts of Jesus are representative spokesmen for the town as a whole. The negative total reaction does not exclude the possibility that there were some exceptions. The fact that Jesus does not do "many" mighty works there indicates that he did do some. In this manner the evangelist hints that there were in Nazareth nonetheless some people who turned to Jesus in faith and asked for his help.

According to the account, it was alien to the thoughts of the Nazarenes that the teaching and mighty acts of Jesus might have some celestial explanation. The evangelist certainly considers that they are blind and obdurate, so that they do not realize (cf. 13: 13—15, 19) that Jesus is a prophet (cf. v. 57), in fact more than a prophet. The man who comes to them is, *according to the evangelist*, the Son of God, equipped with *exousia* from heaven. He comes to his own people but is met with unbelief (ἀπιστία).

The reaction in the home town of Nazareth looks likely to prefigure the final total reaction Jesus meets with in Jerusalem and thus in Israel as a whole. The Nazarenes' question as to where Jesus got his wisdom and mighty acts is rather similar to that of the leaders in Jerusalem as to where he got his *exousia* (21: 23—27).

In the quasi-summary in 11: 2—6, where Jesus answers the question of John the Baptist as to whether he is "the Coming One", it is said, "Blessed is he who takes no offence at me (σκανδαλίζεσθαι)" (cf. 2.3.5.2. above). Obviously, the reaction in Jesus' home town of Nazareth is one of the evangelist's foremost examples of how many took offence at Jesus.

---

[4] Thus Bultmann, *Geschichte* (3: 15), 30—31.

5.2.2. *The unreceptiveness in Chorazin, Bethsaida and Capernaum, 11:20—24 (Lk 10:13—15)*

The pericope of the unrepentant cities gives us first of all the view of Jesus (and of the early Christians) on the unrepentance in the cities where Jesus appears to have been most active. In its form, the pericope is an apothegm: a pronouncement of Jesus with a short narrative introduction. In the latter, the main content of the pronouncement is precisely stated: he rebukes (ὀνειδίζειν) the Galilean towns where he has done most of his mighty acts for not repenting (μετανοεῖν). The pronouncement also states that Chorazin, Bethsaida and Capernaum will be given a harsher judgment than the iniquitous cities of the Old Testament tradition, Tyre, Sidon and Sodom.

This pericope is in many respects similar to the words of judgment on "this generation" in 12:41—42,[5] a pericope which also stems from Q (cf. Lk 11:31—32). In both cases there is a retrospective view, and in both Jesus is assumed to have met with unreceptiveness; in both, a comparison is made with Old Testament examples of Gentiles who are favourably compared with Israel which has now hardened itself against Jesus; and in both there is an allusion to the future judgment where stern justice will be meted out in favour of the Gentiles. The difference between the two pronouncements of Jesus is partly in the form, partly in the question of who is being addressed ("this generation" and three named cities, respectively) and partly in the fact that the rejection in the first case concerns his mighty acts and in the second case his wisdom and preaching. The extensive parallelism reminds us, however, that one should not hold teaching and mighty acts too clearly apart: with both of these Jesus brings the Reign of Heaven close, and with both of them his intention is to bring the people to repentance and acceptance (cf. 4:17 and 11:21 respectively). In both cases the rejection is a rejection of *Jesus*.

Our pericope is of importance because it stems from the Q material; even there Jesus is known as a worker of miracles.[6] It is particularly interesting to note that we are here apparently given important items of historical information. Since the early Christian tradition is otherwise quite silent about Chorazin and has so little to say about Bethsaida, it is difficult to maintain that this pericope was formed during the course of the tradition. Here we appear to be faced with information that we are not given in any other place: Jesus has conducted a thaumaturgical ministry in these two cities.[7]

---

[5] Cf. Fridrichsen, *Problème* (1:13), 49—50, Eng. 75—76.
[6] See, besides this pericope (Mt 11:20—24/Lk 10:13—15), especially Mt 8:5—13/Lk 7:1—10 and Mt 12:22—23/Lk 11:14.
[7] Cf. F. Mussner, *Die Wunder Jesu. Eine Hinführung*, München 1967, 24—33.

Behind the words of judgment against Chorazin, Bethsaida and Capernaum lies the knowledge that the principal reaction to Jesus in these cities has not been receptiveness and faith but unrepentance. As in the Nazareth pericope it is here a question of the total reaction of *entire cities* and not of the attitude of "the crowds" in particular. The blame is presumably laid primarily on the leading men who set the tone in each city.

We have already commented (1.4. above) on the fact that in this pericope we find the term which according to the synoptic tradition Jesus himself used of the miraculous actions he performed, "mighty acts" (δυνάμις, גבורתא). Two further details are worth pointing out: 1. *The theme of belief* — which we met with in the Nazareth pericope — is left out of consideration in this pericope. Here it is presupposed that Jesus has done many mighty acts in cities that have been unrepentant. Here, unbelief has not made this impossible as in Nazareth; 2. According to this pericope Jesus wants to call forth repentance (μετάνοια) with his mighty acts. *The theme of repentance* — which plays its part in the evangelist's total assessment of the reaction of Israel to Jesus' ministry — has not been used in the Matthean adaptation of the individual miracle stories, at least not explicitly, despite the fact that this pericope could have provided a reason to do so.[8]

The pericope of the cities where Jesus has done most of his mighty acts — note especially the home city of Capernaum — also seems to a certain extent to give expression to the theme of the prophet being rejected in his own country. And here too the unreceptiveness in Jerusalem is prefigured and thus the unreceptiveness in official Israel, according to Matthew.

5.3. *The adversaries' polemics*

In the two pericopes we have just examined the fact is commented upon that Jesus has met with unbelief (Nazareth) and unrepentance (Chorazin, Bethsaida and Capernaum) but we are given no intimation of how the adversaries interpreted his mighty acts. If we wish to inform ourselves about this we must go to four of the pericopes of the therapeutic miracles. In two of the cases concerned (9: 32—34, 12: 22—24) the adversaries' reaction is only stated after a short healing narrative; in the latter of these two cases Jesus' defence against their reaction has also been added (12: 25—32). In the two remaining cases the adversaries appear within the actual healing narrative. In the pericope of the healing of the paralytic (9: 1—8) we are informed of the reaction of the adversaries and Jesus'

---

[8] The verb μετανοεῖν occurs 5 times in Matthew (3: 2, 4: 17, 11: 20, 21, 12: 41), the substantive μετάνοια only twice (3: 8, 11). All the cases concern what Israel ought to do when faced with the Baptist and Jesus. In 11: 20—21 and 12: 41 pagan cities are put forward for Israel as examples to be followed.

answer to it in the form of a clearly delimited insertion in the healing narrative. This element of the text angles the rest of the narrative in such a way that this time the healing becomes an action done mainly with the adversaries in mind. Only in the pericope of the healing of the man with the withered hand (12:9—14) has the exchange of opinion with the adversaries been the guiding principle in the narrative as a whole. This pericope may be characterized as a controversy dialogue concerning a case of healing.

5.3.1. *The controversies on the exorcisms*, 9:32—34, 12:22—32 (Mk 3:22—30, Lk 11:14—23, 12:10)

As far as this material is concerned, I shall not discuss the traditio-historical questions here but only point out that the Pharisees' explanation of Jesus' exorcisms (that he drives out demons by Beelzebul) seems to have been handed down in both the Marcan and the Q tradition.

Matthew has compiled his large collection of narratives on Jesus' mighty acts in chaps. 8—9 in such a way that it finally leads on to an intimation of the reactions called forth by Jesus' healing miracles in both the *crowds* and the *Pharisees*.[9] The crowds show an open and positive reaction, the Pharisees one of vehement rejection (9:32—34). The same intimation recurs in 12:22—32, but here the text is supplemented by Jesus' answer to the negative reaction of the Pharisees.

In both cases, the intimations of these two reactions are linked to a briefly sketched item on how Jesus heals a sick person. In 9:32 it is a dumb demoniac, in 12:22 a blind and dumb demoniac. The sick man is led to Jesus, who drives out the demon in the first case so that the sick man is able to speak and heals the man in the second case so that he can both speak and see. This is the basis on which the suggestions are then built up as to the reactions: the *crowds*, firstly, marvel and say, "Never was anything like this seen in Israel" (9:33). They are amazed and say, "Can this be the Son of David?" (12:23). The *Pharisees* on the other hand, say, "He casts out demons by the prince of demons" (9:34) or, "It is only by Beelzebul, the prince of demons, that this man casts out demons" (12:24).

In 12:25—32 there then follows the apology of Jesus (and of the church) in reply to the accusation quoted. This is a *logia* composition of quite a complex nature. Here I shall only consider, fragmentarily, the first four arguments:

1. Vv. 25—26. The thought that one can cast out Satan by Satan is absurd; if this were so the kingdom of Satan could not stand.
2. V. 27. The casting out of demons is also practised in the ranks of the

---

[9] Cf. how the section about the teaching of Jesus (5:1—7:29) ends with some words about the crowd's reaction.

Pharisees. These exorcists can decide whether one can cast out Satan by Satan.

3. V. 28. If it is by the Spirit of God that I cast out demons, then the Reign of God has come upon you.

4. V. 29. The fact that Jesus can plunder Satan's house — to liberate those whom Satan is holding prisoner — must mean that Satan ("the strong man") has met his master ("the stronger man").

The crowds here clothe their reaction in words. Matthew is alone in this. The reaction agrees excellently with the general picture we have met in the material we have examined in chaps. 2—4. The attitude is somewhat unclear and tentative, but it is open and positive and is groping in the right direction. What is particularly remarkable is that we here note the same perspective of the history of salvation as we meet in the decisive pronouncement of Jesus. "Never" has anything like what is now being witnessed been seen in Israel — can this be "the Son of David", that is, the Messiah who has been awaited? This is moving in the direction of Jesus' pronouncement "then the Reign of God has come upon you".

The reaction of the *Pharisees* is simple and clear but negative through and through: Jesus' exorcisms have a satanic background. He stands in the service of Satan, works through his power, and strengthens his reign.

The way in which *Jesus*, and the church, meet this standard objection to the exorcisms involves somewhat heterogeneous elements.[10] The accusation, however, is rejected as absurd, and the positive interpretation of the exorcisms is presented. There are two aspects of this: the Reign of God has approached, and "the stronger man" has bound "the strong man" (Satan).

The *logion* "if it is by the Spirit of God that I cast out demons, then the Reign of God has come upon you" is a traditional pronouncement (belonging to the Q material). Matthew has corrected the wording, altering "the finger of God" to "the Spirit of God".[11] How is this pronouncement to be interpreted?

If one were to take it to mean firstly that Jesus casts out the demons with the Spirit of God as his instrument and secondly that these actions are "signs" that the Reign of God has come, then this *logion* would not stand in agreement with the view presented in the Gospel of Matthew as a whole. Since, however, Matthew has corrected the wording, there is

---

[10] The comparison with the Pharisaic exorcists is an argument without connection with the statement that Jesus' exorcisms reveal the nearness of the Reign of God (v. 28). Otherwise the exorcisms of the Pharisees should be interpreted as manifestations of the Reign as well. Cf. Fridrichsen, *Problème*, 70—76, Eng. 102—110.

[11] The alteration has probably been made in connection with the quotation from Is 42: 1 in verse 18 ("my spirit"). Cf. however R. G. Hamerton-Kelly, A Note on Matthew XII. 28 Par. Luke XI. 20, *New Test. Stud.* 11 (1964—65), 167—169.

every reason to suspect that the logion expresses a conception agreeing with the Matthean perspectives. How should this be interpreted within the framework of the Gospel of Matthew?

The relationship between Jesus and the Spirit — a theme in which Matthew is very interested [12] — is represented as follows: Jesus is conceived in the body of his mother by holy Spirit (1: 18—25). At his baptism the Spirit of God — in its fullness — then comes upon him (3: 13—17). God has thus put his Spirit upon him (12: 18), and he performs his ministry filled by the Spirit. Thus he acts *himself* when he casts out the demons, but he acts filled with the Spirit of God. The relation to the Reign of God is not that the exorcisms are "signs" that the Reign has approached. The exorcism is more than that: it is part of the exercising of the Reign of God. The Reign of God is exercised where the power of Satan is broken.[13] What Jesus is doing is "the works of the Christ" (11: 2), but it could also be called "the works of the Reign". In one way, Matthew seems to identify the Reign of God with the ministry of Jesus. In what he says and does, Jesus is exercising the Reign of God. When Matthew is to reveal the secrets of the Reign it is an important matter to make the *exousia* of Jesus (and of his disciples) clear. We shall return to this later.

5.3.2. *The controversy on the forgiveness of sins*, 9: 1—8 (Mk 2: 1—12, Lk 5: 17—26)

The first clash of all between Jesus and his adversaries in the Gospel of Matthew is on the subject of Jesus' right to forgive sins (9: 1—8). Here already we meet the accusation of blasphemy (βλασφημεῖν), which recurs in a generalized form at the trial before the Sanhedrin (26: 63—68).

The pericope 9: 1—8 has an *inclusio* structure and consists of three main parts:

A. An introduction: a healing narrative, part one, vv. 1—2 (76 syllables);
B. A central part: a dialogue between the adversaries and Jesus, vv. 3—6 b (118 syllables);
C. A conclusion: the healing narrative, part two, vv. 6 c—8 (75 syllables).

If we remove the central part we have a regular healing narrative (A plus C). The persons appearing are Jesus, the sick man and his representatives, and the crowds. The theme of faith is given expression, but only in the narrative text ("when Jesus saw their faith", v. 2), not in the words of Jesus. The latter comprise two pronouncements: he first tells the

---

[12] Matthew only mentions the Spirit in connection with Jesus, except in two borderline cases: 10: 20 (where "the Spirit of your Father" is connected with the testimonies before courts made by the adherents of Jesus) and 22: 43 (David's inspired testimony to the Messiah).

[13] Cf. e.g. R. E. Brown, The Gospel Miracles, in J. L. McKenzie (ed.), *The Bible in Current Catholic Thought*, New York 1962, 186—193.

paralytic that his sins are forgiven and then commands him to rise — healed — and to go home. The narrative is rounded off with a so-called *Chor-Schluss*: the crowds are afraid and glorify God who has given such *exousia* to men.

It is of interest that the healing act of Jesus is in this case divided into two parts: the forgiveness of sins, and the demonstration that the forgiveness has had its effect — that is, that the sickness has vanished. In other words, in the two sayings of Jesus to the paralytic we have *a specific interpretation of what Jesus' healing more precisely means*.

If we now look at the central part (B), we notice that here the actors appearing (the "roles") are only two: Jesus and the adversaries ("some of the scribes", v. 3). The adversaries' objection and criticism is directed at the element of the forgiveness of sins in Jesus' healing ministry: "This man is blaspheming" (v. 3). Jesus reads their thoughts and answers them. The argument about what is "easier" (v. 5) may be taken to mean that the two things belong together and are equally difficult.[14] The remainder of Jesus' pronouncement turns the actual healing to a proof of the *exousia* to forgive sins. The interpretative dialogue in the central part has the effect of rendering the healing in this case a demonstration in front of the adversaries. The healing of the paralytic becomes a "norm miracle" and a "sign" confirming the claim that the Son of man has *exousia* to forgive sins on earth (cf. 1.2. above).[15] In the final words we notice that Matthew does not apprehend this *exousia* as exclusively given to Jesus. It is given to "men", which certainly means *Jesus and the church*.[16]

The pericope of the paralytic gives us an important insight into how Jesus' healings were interpreted by the early Christians and how they were attacked by his adversaries. Against the background of the Old Testament tradition[17] it was natural that these resolute healings, performed without the demand for any form of penance, were apprehended as implying the unconditional forgiveness of sins. It is fully possible that Jesus himself apprehended and intended them in this way, wishing to be he "who forgives all your iniquity, who heals all your diseases" (words from Ps 103: 3). It is also possible, however, that the early Christians, when meditating on and discussing Jesus' unconditional healings, reached this clarity and placed the interpretative words in Jesus' mouth in the narrative of the healing of the paralytic. (I myself consider the former as the more credible alternative.) At all events, even before Mark[18] the

---

[14] Thus Fridrichsen, *Problème*, 92—94, Eng. 130—134.
[15] Cf. also Theissen, *Wundergeschichten*, 118—119, 177.
[16] Thus A. Schlatter, *Der Evangelist Matthäus. Seine Sprache, sein Ziel, seine Selbstständigkeit*⁴, Stuttgart 1957, 301, with reference to 16: 19, and 18: 18.
[17] See K. Stendahl, Gamla Testamentets föreställningar om helandet, *Svensk Exeg. Årsbok* 15 (1950), 5—33.
[18] Cf. Kertelge, *Die Wunder* (Intr.: 3), 75—82.

early Christians saw two elements in Jesus' therapeutic actions: forgiveness and healing. The reaction and polemics of the Jewish scribes, moreover, were directed against the first of these elements. What they found offensive in his healings was not that he made people well but that he did so unconditionally, without demanding confession of sins, repentance and penance.

The theme of the forgiveness of sins takes a very important place in the Gospel of Matthew. When the name of Jesus is interpreted in 1:21, the interpretation is "for he will save his people from their sins". This is not an unaffected, natural phrase that flowed of its own accord from the pen of the evangelist. It is a carefully formed pronouncement showing how he apprehends the *kind* of salvation indicated by the name of Jesus. In the pericope of the last supper (26:28) it is said that the blood of Jesus is poured out for many "for the forgiveness of sins". Matthew is alone in stating it with such definition. It shows what importance he attaches to the forgiveness of sins as an effect of Jesus' death. The saying of the Son of man having come "to serve, and to give his life as a ransom for many" (20:28) has been taken over by Matthew, but it expresses perfectly his view of Jesus' earthly ministry. As a whole, in fact, the theme of forgiveness (God's forgiveness and our forgiveness) and reconciliation plays a strikingly important role in Matthew (cf. further 5:21—26, 38—48, 6:12, 14—15, 12:31—32, 18:15—35).[19]

5.3.3. *The controversy over healing on the sabbath*, 12:9—14 (Mk 3:1—6, Lk 6:6—11)

The sabbath is mentioned only in passing in two places in the Gospel of Matthew (24:20, 28:1), and its problems are treated only in two pericopes (12:1—8, 9—14). In all four places the validity of the sabbath commandment is undisputed.

Essentially, Matthew appears only to be concerned to clarify two questions about the sabbath. The first of these is of a *Christological* nature and concerns Jesus' *exousia* and its relation to the sabbath (12:1—8). Here, the principal rule is: "The Son of man is lord of the sabbath" (v. 8). The second question is of a directly *sabbatological* nature, and concerns what is lawful and what is unlawful on the sabbath (12:9—14). Here, the principal rule given by Jesus is, "So it is lawful to do good on the sabbath" (v. 12).

Since the first of these two pericopes does not concern Jesus' mighty

---

[19] See my article Sacrificial Service and Atonement in the Gospel of Matthew, in *Reconciliation and Hope* (Festschrift in honour of L. L. Morris), Exeter 1974, 25—35, J. S. Kennard, The Reconciliation Tendency in Matthew, *Angl. Theol. Rev.* 28 (1946), 159—163, and Thompson, *Matthew's Advice* (2:25), 175—237.

acts, we shall not comment on it here. The second pericope, however, deserves some amount of commentary at this point.

In Matthew, this pericope (12:9—14) has a stringent structure following the well known *inclusio* pattern. As J. Smit Sibinga has shown, it consists of exactly 200 syllables.[20] The pattern is as follows:

A. An introductory, narrative part, vv. 9—10 (62 syllables);
B. An argumentative part, finishing with the decisive principal rule, vv. 11—12 (62+13 syllables);
C. A concluding narrative part, vv. 13—14 (63 syllables).

As I have already said, the main point is to be found in the decisive rule "So it is lawful to do good on the sabbath" (v. 12). The healing is thus classified as a good work, and such works are declared to be lawful on the sabbath.

The pericope is primarily a controversy dialogue.[21] What is in the foreground is that Jesus is attacked by adversaries ("Pharisees", v. 14; cf. v. 2), who are trying to find points where to attack him (v. 10). The upshot of the controversy is that the Pharisees resolve to destroy him (v. 14). Thus they do not accept his decision that it is lawful to heal on the sabbath.

Consequently, the healing itself is not in the foreground in this pericope. The interpretative dialogue does not in this case concern the power and will of Jesus to heal, nor the faith and will of the sick man to be healed. The dialogue takes place between the *adversaries* and Jesus and concerns the right to heal *on the sabbath*. The sick man is treated almost as demonstration material, as a "case". And the miracle, which is in itself a healing miracle, fulfils the function of a "norm miracle " and, as has already been pointed out (1.2. above), is in fact a "sign" confirming Jesus' *exousia* to heal on the sabbath, even if the term itself is absent.

It is clear that Matthew has toned down the statements in the tradition on Jesus' doing mighty acts on the sabbath. Mark has four pericopes of episodes on the sabbath (1:21—28, 2:23—28, 3:1—6, 6:1—6), and Luke has six (4:16—30, 31—37, 6:1—5, 6—11, 13:10—17, 14:1—6). Matthew places only two of the episodes from Jesus' earthly ministry on a sabbath, and in each case the problem of the sabbath is in the actual centre of the pericope: it is a question of the plucking of the ears of grain on the sabbath (12:1—8) and the right to heal on the sabbath (12:9—14). It is also remarkable that Matthew gives no sign of any reflections on the possibility that Jesus' healings on the sabbath might have a deeper meaning in the history of salvation (as in John) or might reveal the inner secret of the sabbath (as in Mark and Luke). Matthew has turned the edge

---

[20] *Eine literarische Technik* (3:10), 102.
[21] Cf. Bultmann, *Geschichte*, 9.

of the provocative statements in the tradition concerning Jesus' actions on the sabbath, and he does not appear to want to do much more here than to declare and defend the power and right of Jesus (and the church) to heal and perform other "good works" on the sabbath. The attitude is defensive: "it is lawful (ἔξεστιν)".

5.4. *Some conclusions and reflections on the controversy situation*

The pericopes of Jesus' visit to Nazareth and his words of judgement on Chorazin, Bethsaida and Capernaum reveal that Jesus has not been so successful as the idealizing summaries in particular suggest. The critical reflections we noted in chaps. 2—3 above are here confirmed. In our survey we have also established that Matthew, in his adaptation of the *individual miracle narratives*, has not been particularly interested in the two themes of "the prophet and his own country" and "the repentance" (μετανοεῖν), although these themes were obviously of importance to him in his interpretation of Jesus' ministry *as a whole*.

In the two pericopes we are told of unbelief and unrepentance, but we are given no hint of the adversaries' view of Jesus' mighty acts. This *is* given to us, on the other hand, in the four healing narratives which include a suggestion of the reactions of the adversaries to what Jesus is doing. The text tells how the adversaries interpret Jesus' mighty acts and tells of the polemic they mount against them — as Matthew understands the matter. Here we are touching points where it must reasonably be assumed that the evangelist is *aware*. And we have reason to ask one question: Has the concern with the adversaries' polemics affected Matthew's way of presenting Jesus' mighty acts? Has his presentation been given apologetic features?

Before directing this question at the material under discussion, I must repeat one point which as far as I can see is of great importance: *the adversaries only play a small, casual role in the texts on Jesus' miracles.* Confining ourselves to Matthew, we can observe that they are not even mentioned in the summaries nor in the narratives of the non-therapeutic miracles. And as for the fourteen pericopes of the therapeutic miracles, the adversaries are only mentioned in four of these. Their role in three of the pericopes, moreover, seems to be a casual addition to the basic narrative. Thus it is only in one single miracle narrative — or maybe two — that they play a vital role in what is being portrayed. The interpretation of this must be that apologetics was not a primary theme when these narratives took shape and neither was it a main concern of Matthew in his adaptation of the material. Certainly, Matthew wished his readers to know, as it were, what to answer their opponents in a polemic, but he was not so hard pressed as to feel the necessity of repelling the attacks of the adversaries in one pericope after another. It is obvious that the primary driving force behind Matthew's interpretation and presentation of Jesus' mighty acts is the endeavour to reach a positive understanding of the mysteries around Jesus and his *exousia* and the desire to teach the community about them — and not apologetic intentions.

This is the general impression one gains in the concrete material:

1. The point of the polemic against Jesus' *exorcisms* is that they are performed "by the prince of demons". This is a serious accusation, for the punishment for sorcery was death. In 12: 22—32 the evangelist gives an account of the answer of Jesus (and the church) to this polemic. The most important element of this answer is the positive declaration that Jesus is driving out the demons by the Spirit of God, and that this means the Reign of God is at hand.

To what extent has Matthew — and to what extent have his predecessors — allowed the concern with this accusation and this polemic from authoritative Jewish adversaries to affect the presentation of Jesus' exorcisms?

We have seen that Matthew alters the picture of Jesus as an exorcist to a broader picture of Jesus as the healer of Israel in a more general meaning. He reduces the number of exorcistic narratives and deletes rough-hewn, popular strains in the tradition to the extent to which they occur. This may to some extent be influenced by apologetic considerations; in some of Mark's pericopes, Jesus somewhat resembles a Hellenistic thaumaturge.[22] There is no doubt at all, however, that the main reason is that Matthew apprehends Jesus as the Son of God, filled by the Spirit of God and equipped with divine authority: the Father has delivered all things to him. The main reason for Matthew portraying the healing Jesus as so high and all-powerful is of course that he has this positive picture of Christ. Jesus had to heal in a manner befitting "the Son of the Living God".

2. The main concern of the adversaries' polemic against Jesus' *healings of other types* is that they include an unconditional forgiveness of sins, which only God can grant: Jesus is *blaspheming* when he forgives sins in this way. This is a serious accusation, for the punishment for blasphemy was death. In 9: 1—8, the evangelist gives an account of the answer of Jesus (and the church) to this criticism. This answer, in a nutshell, seems to be that the very fact of the healing shows that the power and the right to forgive sins has been given to "men" — that is, to Jesus and the church.

To what extent has Matthew — and to what extent have his predecessors — allowed the concern with this polemic to affect the presentation of Jesus' healings?

One noteworthy fact must be underlined: the explicit emphasizing of the forgiveness of sins is not a *typical* aspect of the synoptic narratives of

---

[22] Especially Mk 7: 31—37, 8: 22—26; see 3: 19 above.

Jesus' healings. This is only found in the pericope of the healing of the paralytic. Can this mean that the evangelists and their predecessors have been influenced by the Pharisees' polemic and have toned down this aspect? The answer is no. There is nothing to suggest that the early Christians temporized with their *exousia* to forgive sins or avoided speaking of it. It was held fast and justified. The reason for this theme not being rendered explicit in a series of healing narratives is probably that it was sufficient for it to be expressed in one pericope — and one that was surely considered to be highly important! This concrete example was enough to demonstrate the general consideration — which was not a new one — that healing included the forgiveness of sins. There were other themes which — for various reasons — needed to be emphasized over and over again in the narratives of Jesus' healings.

3. The adversaries also attacked the fact that Jesus *healed on the sabbath.* The accusation, as formulated, is serious, for the punishment for breaking the sabbath was death. The synoptists say, too, that the Pharisees' original decision to destroy Jesus was based on the fact that he healed on the sabbath.[23] In 12: 1—14, Matthew gives an account of the answer of Jesus (of the church) to this criticism. This is firstly that Jesus is lord of the sabbath and secondly that the healings are good works, which are lawful on the sabbath.

To what extent has Matthew — and to what extent have his predecessors — allowed the concern with this criticism on the part of the adversaries to influence the presentation of Jesus' healing?

One thing is clear — Matthew has toned down the statements in the tradition concerning Jesus' healing on the sabbath. It is not entirely unlikely that apologetic considerations played a part here. In this case as well, however, we should certainly look primarily for a positive main reason. This is, in this case, that Matthew and his church obviously respected the sabbath commandment and were loth to undermine its authority. Their positive attitude was that Jesus had remained loyal to this commandment but had made its real meaning clear: the sabbath commandment is no obstacle to "good works" and consequently, it is no obstacle to healings.

Our survey of the above presented material concerning opposition and controversies has confirmed the view we already held, namely that apologetic considerations do not seem to have played any important role for Matthew when formulating the text sections on Jesus' mighty acts. His main intention was positive: to clarify and present what he has "understood" (συνιέναι). The controversy material does not add much to the picture we have been given by the positive material. Even so, however, a meagre result can be *important*.

[23] Mk 3: 1—6, Mt 12: 9—14; cf. Lk 6: 6—11.

6. The Christological appellations in our material

To conclude, we shall note some observations and reflections concerning Christology in our material. By "our material" I mean in this chapter the summaries and miracle narratives (both therapeutic and non-therapeutic). On those occasions when I consider the special controversy material (11: 20—24, 13: 54—58) or other material on the borders of "our" material, I shall state this separately.

There is little cause to try to write a summary of the type that might be entitled "the Christology of the Matthean miracle narratives". When the Gospel was finally edited, the Matthean church members had a synthetic, many-faceted picture of Christ, a picture which was illustrated with many kinds of material. This material included the summaries and concrete miracle narratives as elements among others. To isolate them — within the Gospel of Matthew — and to write their "Christology" seems to me a far-fetched and artificial undertaking.

It is, however, reasonable to ask how "Jesus Christ, the son of the Living God" is actually portrayed in our material and what contribution is made by these elements of the Gospel of Matthew to the total picture of him. I shall do this, but limit myself to making a few comments concerning the *Christological appellations* that are to be found in our material. This is done in an open and fragmentary manner.

6.1. *Jesus, the Christ, "the Coming One"*

The Christological appellations upon which we shall comment in this chapter are "the Son of man", "the Lord", "the Son of David", "the Son of God" and "the Servant of God". First however, we shall say a few words about the name of Jesus, the title of Messiah/Christ and the enigmatic appellation "the Coming One".[1]

The central figure of the Gospel bears the name of *Jesus*. It is surely inescapable that when the Gospel was finally edited this name had long since gained considerable Christological overtones. Even the very signi-

---

[1] For a recent and fresh discussion of all the Christological designations in Matthew, see J. D. Kingsbury, *Matthew: Structure, Christology, Kingdom*, Philadelphia 1975, 40—127. Cf. F. Hahn's impressive book *Christologische Hoheitstitel. Ihre Geschichte im frühen Christentum*², Göttingen 1964 and H. R. Balz, *Methodische Probleme der neutestamentlichen Christologie*, Neukirchen-Vluyn 1967.

ficance of the name suggested this (cf. 1: 21). It is important to underline, however, that "Jesus" is first and last the name of a person, and that it has only gained Christological connotations.[2] When Matthew tells of the earthly Jesus he uses this name almost without exception. None of the titles has been able to displace it. Jesus is a figure of flesh and blood with an individual human name (cf. 2.7. above). This is the case in our material as well.

The title of Messiah/Christ would be worth a lengthy study. It was so important that it soon grew stereotyped as Jesus' second name (note this in Mt 1: 1, 18; the reading Χριστός in 16: 21 is hardly original), although to begin with it posed several different problems. For Matthew it is a matter of course that Jesus is the Messiah. We need not go further into this point. In our material, however, we only meet the term in one quasi-summary, in the expression "the works of the Christ" (11: 2). We have already pointed out that this formulation seems to have been chosen because the allusion is not merely to what Jesus does but also to what the disciples do in his name, the Messianic mighty works (cf. 1.3. and 2.3.5.2. above).

The enigmatic designation "the Coming One (ὁ ἐρχόμενος)" only occurs in one place in Matthew, and this is in our material, in the context just mentioned (11: 3); cf. "he who comes in the name of the Lord" in 21: 9 and "your king is coming" in 21: 5. The pericope in 11: 2—6 with its parallels shows that this designation — at least in the Q tradition, in Matthew and Luke — was associated with the expected time of salvation and its wonderful events. To judge by the type, it was one of those enigmatic terms which the scribes tended to consider particularly significant in the old texts and to apprehend as an allusion to the Messiah.

6.2. *The Son of man*

The designation "the Son of man" (ὁ υἱὸς τοῦ ἀνθρώπου) occurs in only one place in our material. To preclude unfounded conclusions *e silentio* I shall actualize two observations on the use of language in the synoptic gospels.

1. The evangelists themselves never use the designation "the Son of man" when telling of Jesus. Thus the fact that this expression does not occur in the material telling of Jesus' mighty acts does not say anything *special*.

2. The designation "the Son of man" only occurs in pronouncements of Jesus, where it always refers — according to the evangelists — to Jesus himself. These first-person pronouncements are never concerned with who Jesus *is*, but they do concern *a.* his position and situation, his powers and

---

[2] See A. Deissmann, The Name 'Jesus', in G. K. A. Bell & A. Deissmann (ed.), *Mysterium Christi*, London, New York & Toronto 1930, 3—27, cf. Kingsbury, *ibidem*, 84—85.

tasks at the present time, *b.* his imminent passion, death and resurrection, and *c.* his future appearance in heaven at the time of judgment.³

Where — with this in mind — can we *expect* the appellation "the Son of man" in our material? This should be in the pronouncements of Jesus on his mighty acts, i.e. in the dialogues within the miracle narratives and in such pericopes as 11: 2—6 or 12: 22—32. In the controversy material, we might expect the expression in 11: 20—24 and 13: 54—58.

What we find, however, is not much — only one single instance. In the pericope of the paralytic (9: 1—8) Jesus says: "The Son of man has authority on earth to forgive sins" (v. 6). This *logion* is reminiscent of the declaration in 12: 8: "The Son of man is lord of the sabbath." In each case the pronouncement is of a defensive nature. It claims that what Jesus is doing lies within the compass of the Son of man's *exousia*. He has authority both to do good works on the sabbath and to forgive sins (cf. 5.3.3. and 5.5. above).

In neither of these cases are we dealing with a mistranslation, where the pronouncement in its original form would have referred to mankind in general.⁴ We do see, on the other hand, in 9: 8 that "the Son of man" is an appellation that is, so to speak, open towards the church: "the saints" of the Son of man (cf. Dan 7: 13—18) share in his *exousia*. The same is probably implied in the pronouncement on the sabbath in 12: 8.

The *logion* in 20: 28 may perhaps be said to lie at the borders of our material: "the Son of man came . . . to serve (διακονεῖν)". This seems to refer to Jesus' whole way of shaping his ministry, including the serving that consists of healing (θεραπεύειν). And this pronouncement as well is open towards the followers of Jesus. When the Son of man "serves" he is an example for those who would follow him (note the ὥσπερ).⁵

We note that in our material there is only one pronouncement including the designation "the Son of man". It is, of course, important (cf. 5.3.2. and 5.4. above) but nonetheless it does stand alone. It seems as if the motif of the Son of man is combined only in a secondary and weak manner with the traditions of Jesus' concrete healings and other concrete mighty acts during his earthly ministry. The theme of the *Reign of God* takes a more outstanding place in our material.

---

³ Cf. R. Bultmann, *Theologie des Neuen Testaments*⁷, Tübingen 1977, 30—33. See from the discussion R. Leivestad, Exit the Apocalyptic Son of Man, *New Test. Stud.* 18 (1971—72), 243—267, B. Lindars, Re-Enter the Apocalyptic Son of Man, *ibidem* 22 (1975—76), 52—72, C. F. D. Moule, *The Origin of Christology*, London, New York & Melbourne 1977, 11—22.

⁴ So e.g. T. W. Manson, *The Teaching of Jesus*, Cambridge 1951, 213—214.

⁵ See my article *Gottes Sohn* (Intr.: 7), 84—88.

6.3. *The Lord* (Kyrios)

Several scholars are inclined to conceive of ὁ Κύριος ("the Lord") as the primary Christological title in the Gospel of Matthew.[6] As Kingsbury has correctly pointed out,[7] this point of view is untenable. The designation κύριος was far too vague and general to enable it to play this role. It is typical that in the synoptic gospels we may search in vain for questions of the type "Are you, is this, the Lord (ὁ Κύριος)?" It is also typical that we do not even find pronouncements of confession such as "You are, this is, the Lord!" *Kyrios* was not a distinctive appellation.

Our point of departure must be that the title of Lord was very general and highly flexible, especially in the vocative form. It was used by the slave to his master, often enough by the son to his father (cf. 21: 29), by simple people to those of distinction, by the people to those in authority and rulers, and by mortals to God. Thus the *dignity* of the appellation was a shifting one.[8]

It seems to me groundless to take Mt 7: 21—22, 25: 37, 44 as substantiation for the assertion that the title as a designation of Jesus primarily belonged to eschatological contexts.[9] The use of language in these scenes of judgment is simple and obvious. How else would one — as a righteous or unrighteous person — address one's judge if not with the title "Lord"?

The dignity must be determined from case to case by means of a detailed analysis of each pericope, paying attention to the context, motives, phraseology and so forth. It is clear that for Matthew the address *Kyrie* is a *positive* one. As many commentators have pointed out, Matthew never makes Jesus' adversaries address him thus.[10] This tells us nothing, however, about the potency of this form of address in the individual case. One must ask oneself each time how great insight into the secret of Jesus and how great veneration the evangelist may reasonably be supposed to ascribe to the persons who in various contexts call Jesus "Lord".

In our material we see that the disciples call Jesus *Kyrie* in the two non-therapeutic miracle narratives that contain any word of address (the calming of the storm, 8: 25, and the walking on the water, 14: 28, 30). Here the main question is how great insight into the secret of Jesus the disciples have on these occasions — according to Matthew.

---

[6] So e.g. W. Trilling, *Das wahre Israel* (2: 17), 21—51, and H. Frankemölle, *Jahwebund und Kirche Christi*, Münster 1975, passim. See the discussion in Kingsbury, *Matthew*, 103—113.

[7] *ibidem*.

[8] Cf. already W. Bousset, *Kyrios Christos. Geschichte des Christusglaubens von den Anfängen des Christentums bis Irenaeus*², Göttingen 1921, 78—79.

[9] Thus G. Strecker, *Der Weg der Gerechtigkeit. Untersuchungen zur Theologie des Matthäus*², Göttingen 1966, 123—126.

[10] Thus G. Bornkamm, Enderwartung und Kirche im Matthäusevangelium, in *Überlieferung*, 38—39, followed by many.

In the stories of the therapeutic miracles we find that the supplicants address Jesus as *Kyrios* in all the pericopes where some form of address occurs, namely: the leper (8: 2), the Roman centurion (8: 6, 8), two blind men (9: 28), two other blind men (20: 30, 31), the Canaanite woman (15: 22, 25, 27), and the father of the epileptic boy (17: 15). In every case the person speaking reveals a positive faith in Jesus, treating him as a person with the power to help, a person with *exousia*, a saviour — in other words, as his benefactor and *lord*. It is hardly likely that Matthew knew of any positive associations here with a thaumaturge or θεῖος ἀνήρ in Hellenistic style.[11] Neither would it show any great sensitivity to the text, however, to read some full-toned "*Kyrios* Christology" into the cries of these supplicants to Jesus. We may suppose that the evangelist had no kind of need to delimit the significance of the term in these narratives. It was open to humbler or more elevated interpretation, and the evangelist seems to have meant that these people in search of help were on the right track without realizing anything like the whole truth about Jesus (cf. 5.3.1. above).

In three of these cases we see that the title of *Kyrios* is combined with the title "the Son of David" (9: 27—31, 15: 21—28, 20: 29—34). This produces a certain amount of exactitude, but only a certain amount. The positive interpretation of the person of Jesus is still *vague and unclear*. We shall notice this when we now take a close look at how the title "the Son of David" is used.

6.4. *The Son of David*

None of the evangelists shows such interest in the Son of David theme as Matthew.[12] In John the appellation is not found at all. In Mark and Luke we find it in two pericopes — in the story of the blind man near Jericho (Mk 10: 46—52, Lk 18: 35—43), and in the controversy dialogue on the question of the Son of David (Mk 12: 35—37, Lk 20: 41—44). Matthew does have these two pericopes (20: 29—34 and 22: 41—46). But he has

---

[11] On the broad discussion about the Hellenistic "divine man", see L. Bieler's basic work, ΘΕΙΟΣ ΑΝΗΡ. *Das Bild des "göttlichen Menschen" in Spätantike und Frühchristentum*, 2 vols., Wien 1935—1936, D. L. Tiede, *The Charismatic Figure as Miracle Worker*, Missoula 1972, C. H. Holladay, '*Theios Aner' in Hellenistic Judaism*, Missoula 1977, Theissen, *Wundergeschichten* (Intr.: 2), 262—264, 268—273, and O. Betz, The Concept of the So-Called Divine Man in Mark's Christology, in *Studies in New Testament and Early Christian Literature* (Festschrift in honour of A. P. Wikgren), Leiden 1972, 229—240.

[12] See C. Burger, *Jesus als Davidssohn. Eine traditionsgeschichtliche Untersuchung*, Göttingen 1970, 72—106, and cf. J. M. Gibbs, Purpose and Pattern in Matthew's Use of the Title 'Son of David', *New Test Stud*. 10 (1963—64), 446—464, J. Fitzmyer, The Son of David Tradition and Matt. 22.41—46 and Parallels, *Concilium* 20 (1966), 40—46, Kingsbury, *Matthew*, 99—103, idem, The Title "Son of David" in Matthew's Gospel, *Journ. of Bibl. Lit.* 95 (1976), 591—602. See further note 14 below.

also inserted the designation "the Son of David" in seven additional places, in one of these cases as an appellation for Joseph (1: 20) and in the others as an appellation for Jesus. These are in the genealogy (1: 1), in the cry of the two blind men for mercy in 9: 27 (a doublet of 20: 30, 31), in the plea for help of the Canaanite woman (15: 22), in the reaction of the crowds (12: 23), and in the cries of Hosanna of the crowds and the children (21: 9 and 15 respectively).

It is quite clear that the Son of David theme is important for Matthew. It is also quite clear that it has an obvious link with Jesus' *healing*. In our material we notice that Matthew has taken up from the tradition (Mark; cf. Luke) the pericope of the blind man near Jericho who addresses Jesus as "Son of David". In Matthew there are two blind men and they cry twice: "Lord (κύριε), have mercy on us, Son of David (υἱὸς Δαυίδ)!" (20: 30, 31).[13] In the doublet in 9: 27, two other blind men cry in the same way (once). As well as this, the Canaanite woman in 15: 22 cries: "Have mercy on me, O Lord, Son of David (κύριε υἱὸς Δαυίδ)!" In none of these three pericopes do we find "Son of David" alone as an address; it is combined with "Lord". The designation does occur alone, however, in another place, 12: 23, where Jesus heals a blind and dumb demoniac; the crowds' reaction to this is expressed in the question: "Can this be the Son of David (ὁ υἱὸς Δαυίδ)?" The cry of Hosanna in 21: 15 also seems to have a connection with Jesus' healing (21: 14).

There is no reason here to deal in greater detail with the present debate on the Matthean "Son of David" Christology, for example the questions of whether this is a special allusion to ancient expectations of a *royal* Messiah of the house of David and whether the theme of Solomon as exorcist played a part.[14] It may be pertinent, however, to point out once more that in the Gospel of Matthew Jesus the Son of David is not primarily an exorcist but the healer of Israel in a more general sense, and also that his healings are part of his serving ministry in Israel. Jesus the Son of David humbles himself and serves his people.[15]

Above all I would like to underline that the title "Son of David" is by no means the foremost title in the first gospel for the earthly Jesus.

---

[13] N.b., however, the text-critical problems, B. M. Metzger, *A Textual Commentary on the Greek New Testament*, London & New York 1971, 53—54.

[14] See L. R. Fisher, "Can This Be the Son of David?", in *Jesus and the Historian* (Festschrift in honour of E. C. Colwell), Philadelphia 1968, 82—97, E. Lövestam, Davidsson-kristologin hos synoptikerna, *Svensk Exeg. Årsbok* 37—38 (1972—73), 196—210, K. Berger, Die königlichen Messiastraditionen des Neuen Testaments, *New Test. Stud.* 20 (1973—74), 1—44, D. C. Duling, Solomon, Exorcism, and the Son of David, *Harv. Theol. Rev.* (1975), 235—252, idem, *The Therapeutic Son of David* (2: 11).

[15] The ideal that the successor of David and Solomon should "serve" (עבד, δουλεύειν) his people is expressed in 1 Kings 12: 7.

There are scholars who think so.[16] This — as Kingsbury has shown [17] — is not the case at all. The role played by the title in the Matthean material is important, but it is limited.

The clearest indication of this in our material is the fact that it is not the followers, the disciples, who address Jesus in this way but simple, ignorant outsiders: a heathen woman, four blind men in Israel, the crowds, the children in the temple. Jesus is not identified in this way by his disciples (although these do not, naturally, reject the thought that he is the Son of David). And the adversaries, the leading men of Israel, do not enter into dispute with him about *this* title (cf. 22: 41—46). It is not the decisive appellation.

For Matthew, the title "Son of David" naturally says important things about Jesus, linking him with many Messianic words of the prophets. According to him, however, it gives only a very roughly correct picture of Jesus — it only says a superficial part of the truth about him.[18] This is also true in those cases where it is complemented with the title "Lord". Even these two appellations in combination only give a preliminary insight into the secret of Jesus according to Matthew.

6.5. *The Son of God and the Servant of God*

For Matthew and his church Jesus is "the Christ, the Son of the Living God". This is the confession of Peter, the foremost spokesman of the church, in Mt 16: 16. And it is this claim — the most objectionable part of which lies in the qualified designation "the Son of God" — which is rejected by the leaders of Israel and those who follow along with them: they call it blasphemy, deserving death (26: 63—66) and mock at it (26: 67—68, 27: 41—43).

For Matthew, "the Son of God ([ὁ] υἱὸς [τοῦ] θεοῦ)" is the most important Christological title, that which best indicates the secret of the person of Jesus.[19] This appellation has become so familiar that it can at times — in an almost Johannine fashion — be abbreviated to "the Son" (11: 27, [21: 38,] 24: 36, 28: 19).[20] "The Son of God" is not treated as a ready-made title for a specific figure for which people are simply waiting and with which Jesus is merely identified. It is used as an *interpretative* designation, a designation intended to reveal who exactly the enigmatic Jesus actually is. The objectionable aspect is that the appellation

---

[16] Thus e.g. G. Strecker, R. Hummel und A. Suhl; see the discussion in Kingsbury, *Matthew*, 99—103.
[17] *ibidem*.
[18] According to Kingsbury, the Matthean use of the title is determined by apologetic reasons as well: Matthew uses it in order to underline the guilt that devolves upon Israel for not receiving its Messiah, *ibidem*. Cf. also Duling, *The Therapeutic Son*.
[19] 2: 15, 3: 17, 8: 29, 16: 16, 17: 5, 21: 37, 26: 63; and 11: 27, 21: 38, 24: 36, 28: 19. See my *Gottes Sohn*; and Kingsbury, *Matthew*, 42—83.
[20] For another opinion, see Hahn, *Christologische Hoheitstitel*, 319—333.

— which is flexible — is taken in such a qualified sense and applied to a Messianic figure whom the leading men of Israel, headed by the Sanhedrin, reject as a criminal and condemn to death.

For Matthew, Jesus is the Son of God in the fullest sense already in his mother's womb. He is conceived by holy Spirit (1: 18, 20); he only becomes the Son of *David* by the fact of his "adoption" by Joseph. At his baptism he receives the full measure of the Spirit of God (3: 16) and conducts his subsequent ministry filled with the Spirit (12: 18, 28). (Cf. 5.3.1. above.)

Thus he is the Son of God by his very parentage and by his endowments. Matthew is also concerned to show that this sonship to God has been *revealed from heaven*. "No one knows the Son except the Father" (11: 27); this is why the Father must reveal who Jesus is. Joseph is given to know (in a dream) by an angel of the Lord that the child Jesus is of holy Spirit (1: 20). At his baptism, the voice from heaven (the Father's voice) confirms that Jesus is the beloved, chosen Son of God (3: 17). On the mountain of transfiguration the three leading disciples hear the heavenly voice give the same testimony as to who Jesus is and also recommend him (17: 5). When Peter confesses that Jesus is "the Christ, the Son of the living God", Jesus says that he has not been given this insight in a normal, human manner but that it has been revealed to him by the Father in heaven (16: 17).[21]

Matthew confirms Jesus' sonship to God, however, in another way as well, a way which in one respect is most important. He is concerned to show that throughout his entire ministry Jesus legitimated himself as the Son of God by being the *servant* of God, at one with God and *obedient to God* in everything, in his "strength" as well as in his "weakness". This is presented explicitly and programmatically in certain pericopes: the temptation narrative, the Gethsemane pericope and the crucifixion narrative. Matthew tries to show this, however, in the Gospel in its entirety. The whole of Jesus' ministry takes place "according to the scriptures". In everything, he fulfils the demands of *the law* — with his whole heart and with his whole soul and with all his resources[22] — and in everything he is and does and says, as in everything that happens to him, the words *of the prophets* are fulfilled. The so-called formula quotations show quite explicitly how very concerned Matthew is to demonstrate how the whole story of Jesus agrees with "what was said (by God, in the law and the prophets) (τὸ ῥηθέν)". This matter also appears very clearly, however, if one studies the way in which the evangelist touches up and shapes his material in other respects.

The theme of the Son of God, for the reasons indicated above, has a strong

---

[21] The Matthean Jesus gives, however, rather clear hints himself, 11: 25—27, 21: 33—43, 22: 1—14, 41—46.
[22] This I have tried to elucidate in a number of studies; see esp. *Gottes Sohn*, and "*med hela ditt hjärta*". *Om Bibelns ethos*, Lund 1979, 35—62.

natural anchorage in *epiphanic* texts such as the baptism narrative, the transfiguration pericope and the Galilean resurrection story. Thus we need not be surprised when we go to "our material" to find this theme in stories of the *non-therapeutic* miracles — that is, those among the miracle stories that are of a more or less clearly epiphanic character. The double narrative of how Jesus and Peter walk on the water leads into the confession of the disciples: "Truly you are the Son of God" (14: 22—33). This double pericope does have the character of an epiphany. The title "the Son of God" is not expressed but is probably suggested in the pericope of the calming of the storm, which is also a kind of epiphany miracle. "The men" wonder: "Of what sort (ποταπός) is this [man], that even winds and sea obey him?" (8: 23—27). The theme of the Son of God also occurs in the pericope of the coin: those who are to be accorded the privilege of being helped by the miracle are "the Sons (of God)", Jesus and Peter (17: 24—27).

The theme of the Son of God has hardly any anchorage, on the other hand, in the pericopes of the *therapeutic* miracles, if these are to be taken at their face value. None of the healing narratives leads on to people wondering whether Jesus is the son of God or to a confession that he is. The statements on the great amazement and stir caused by Jesus' therapeutic works (9: 8, 33, 12: 23, 15: 31) may perhaps lead one's thoughts in this direction, but the actual designation is absent and cannot be said with any degree of certainty to be implied. Only in one pericope do we find it: the narrative concerning the two demoniacs in Gadara (8: 28—34). Here, however, the secret of Jesus is stated even before the miracle, and not because of it. The demons call him "Son of God" (υἱὲ τοῦ θεοῦ). This, of course, is not an address of veneration and honour. The words are calculated to reveal that the demons know his secret. With their supernatural vision they see what human eyes find hard to see. The attempt to overpower Jesus that perhaps originally lay in the words of the demons has almost certainly lost its colour for Matthew. What he finds in the words, we may assume, is that the demons, against their will, give testimony to the real identity of Jesus.[23] He is not a man of Beelzebul, he is the Son of God (cf. 12: 24—29) who has come to them "before the time".

The narratives of Jesus' healings portray the immense power of Jesus; people marvel. This feature of the narratives is open toward various types of High Christology, and plausibly even to Christology of the Son of God. As we have seen, however, the actual designation "the *Son* of God" only crops up in one case, which is a special one: the pericope of the demons in Gadara. Matthew does, on the other hand, very clearly associate Jesus' healing with the theme of the *Servant* (ὁ παῖς) of God.[24]

---

[23] Cf. Fridrichsen, *Problème* (1: 13), 77—79, Eng. 111—113, idem, Jesu kamp mot de urene ånder, *Svensk Teol. Kvartalskr.* 5 (1929), 299—303. See also O. Bauernfeind, *Die Worte der Dämonen im Markusevangelium*, Stuttgart 1927.
[24] Cf. Held, *Matthäus* (Intr.: 4), 246—252.

Matthew does not link any of his formula quotations to any concrete healing narrative. He does, however, provide two of his *summaries* of Jesus' healings with a formula quotation: 8: 16—17 and 12: 15—21. The Christological designation is "the Servant of God" or "my Servant" (ὁ παῖς τοῦ θεοῦ, ὁ παῖς μου). It should, perhaps, be said that the Son of God and the Servant of God are hardly two clearly differentiated designations for Matthew: παῖς does mean not only "servant" but also "boy", "son". Both quotations are taken from the texts on the Servant of God in the Book of Isaiah (53: 4 and 42: 1—4 respectively). In the first quotation mentioned (Mt 8: 17), the actual designation "my Servant" is only implied, but it is unambiguously implied, for in Is 53: 4 οὗτος refers back to ὁ παῖς μου in 52: 13. In the second quotation (Mt 12: 18) the term is expressly stated.

It is of some interest to see what is Matthew's purpose in using these quotations. What he is emphasizing with these two quotations is not Jesus' *sovereignty* (even if he does assume this, cf. 12: 18); what he is intending to show is that Jesus' *humility and serving* are in agreement with the scriptures: that he takes upon himself the infirmities and takes away the diseases, that he acts quietly and discreetly, takes care of those who are small and weak, and becomes a hope of the nations. (See further 2.3.2. above.)

6.6. *Concluding remarks*

Each of the different Christological appellations in "our material" has its own importance, by virtue of its basic meaning and its rich associations. And yet it still seems as if the importance of these appellations in "our material" were limited. They are only inserted sporadically and they say less than one might expect. In the *majority* of the miracle narratives there is no explicit Christological title, and in the summaries there is none at all, just the name of Jesus. The designation that carries the greatest weight ("the Son of God"), and which has a natural right of existence in the pericopes of the non-therapeutic miracles, only occurs in a single healing narrative (an exorcistic one). Its companion-piece ("the Servant of God") does not occur in any of the miracle narratives at all. It does, on the other hand, occur — once explicitly and once implicitly — in formula quotations associated with two summaries, and it has therefore a great interpretative value. The Christological appellations occurring most frequently in the miracle narratives ("Lord", and "Lord, Son of David") only tell us a superficial part of the "truth" about Jesus.

Thus the element in our material that speaks most strongly and clearly is not the Christological appellations. It is the actual interpretative portrayal of what sort of a person Jesus is and of what he does. In the preceding chapters we have been able to establish that the most important interpretative elements in the narratives are the dialogue elements they contain: the words of the supplicants and — above all — the words of Jesus. In the dialogues a very clear statement is made on the one hand of Jesus' unlimited resources of power (his *exousia*) and of his will (his *thelein*) to have mercy and to serve; and on the other hand of the faith that is required on the part of the supplicants among the people and even more on the part of his disciples, these men who — with *exousia* from him and in his name — are to continue his work on earth every day until the end of time.

Conclusion: The mighty acts of Jesus according to Matthew

I shall not make any actual summary of the observations and reflections presented above. The most important ones are easily found at the end of each chapter — and some observations as to the *form* of the material in 3.3., 4.2., 5.3.2. and 5.3.3. above. To conclude with, however, I shall give a brief survey, sketched in broad outline, of how Matthew presents the mighty acts of Jesus.

Matthew identifies Jesus of Nazareth as "the Messiah, the Son of the Living God". In earlier studies I have attempted to show how Matthew portrays the activity of Jesus in Israel as a ministry in two phases. During the first of these, God is with him: he is active in "strength". During the second — which is short — God has delivered him over and abandoned him: he is placed in a position of "weakness". The mighty acts which Matthew ascribes to Jesus are all performed during the first phase. Jesus appears in Israel as a man with sensational ἐξουσία (authority and power): he performs marvellous, powerful acts, δυνάμεις (Chapter 1 above). It appears that Matthew very consciously divides these into two types — I have called them here therapeutic and non-therapeutic miracles respectively — and interprets them for two different theological purposes.

Jesus teaches and preaches the gospel of the Reign — something about which I have not written in this book — and he heals sick people and casts out evil spirits. He behaves with incomparable *exousia* as *the healer of Israel*. It is very striking how the Matthean summaries bring out the therapeutic aspect of Jesus' ministry in Israel (Chapter 2 above). This part of Jesus' ministry is not directed towards the disciples but outwards: Jesus heals the crowds and their sick.

In the material concerning individual cases, too, the therapeutic miracles are directed towards outsiders — people who are not (yet) disciples. With their strong desire to understand (συνιέναι) the secrets of Jesus, Matthew and his circle have worked with these narratives and attempted to grasp and lay bare the secret of Jesus' "wisdom" (σοφία) and "mighty acts" (δυνάμεις). In these pericopes Matthew brings out very clearly the *exousia* of Jesus and its relationship to the faith (πιστεύειν) of the persons who are in need (Chapter 3 above).

Jesus' *exousia* and the faith of men are also the central themes in the material on Jesus' other mighty acts — the non-therapeutic miracles. These, however, are worked throughout for the disciples. Here new secrets concerning Jesus' incomparable *exousia* are revealed, and the faith on which light is shed is the faith needed by Jesus' disciples to be able to discharge Jesus' *exousia* and perform mighty acts themselves in his name (Chapter 4 above).

In rendering and interpreting the tradition, Matthew has been highly conscious of the fact that Jesus met with disfavour and that his public appearance and works were interpreted unfavourably and rendered suspect by his adversaries in Israel. Despite this, however, it does not seem that the evangelist's presentation of Jesus' miracles has been particularly strongly affected by apologetic intentions (Chapter 5 above).

Matthew's aim was to present Jesus clearly and simply as the one who fulfils innumerable prophecies of the coming time of salvation and can be identified by the aid of *many* old designations of exaltedness. Above all he is, however, "the Messiah, the Son of the Living God", whose genuineness has shown itself in the fact that he has taken it upon himself to be in all things — in his "strength" as well as in his "weakness" — "the Servant of God" (Chapter 6 above).

www.ingramcontent.com/pod-product-compliance
Lightning Source LLC
Chambersburg PA
CBHW060423090426
42734CB00011B/2428